iOS 5 Essentials

Harness iOS 5's new powerful features to create
stunning applications

Steven F. Daniel

PUBLISHING

BIRMINGHAM - MUMBAI

iOS 5 Essentials

First published: January 2012

Production Reference: 1170112

Published by Packt Publishing Ltd.
Livery Place
35 Livery Street
Birmingham B3 2PB, UK.

ISBN 978-1-84719-226-7

www.packtpub.com

Cover Image by Evelyn lam (yeeyean@gmail.com)

Credits

Author
Steven F. Daniel

Reviewers
Cory Bohon

John Dometita

Richard England

Chris Gummer

Thanh Huynh

Robb Lewis

Dan Lingman

Acquisition Editor
Wilson D'souza

Lead Technical Editor
Shreerang Deshpande

Technical Editor
Lubna Shaikh

Project Coordinator
Alka Nayak

Proofreader
Lydia May Morris

Indexer
Rekha Nair

Graphics
Manu Joseph

Production Coordinator
Alwin Roy

Cover Work
Alwin Roy

Foreword

Apple's iOS platform, with iPads, iPhones, and iPod touches is the hottest thing in software development right now. An exquisite OS and hardware demands great development tools, and Apple has provided those tools in the form of Xcode. Xcode, just like iOS, is built with ease-of-use in the mind.

Whether you're new to iOS development, or a seasoned pro, this book will guide you through developing in iOS 5 and Xcode 4 with the same ease-of-use that Xcode is known for. It's like this book and iOS 5 development were meant for each other.

Just like Xcode 4, iOS 5 has a lot of new development features, including one of the most-anticipated feature-iCloud. With iCloud, you can store your application's files and settings in the cloud. This book covers these great new features.

With this book, you'll be developing for iOS 5 and using Xcode 4's newest features in no time.

Cory Bohon

About the Author

Steven F. Daniel is originally from London, England, but lives in Australia.

He is the owner and founder of GenieSoft Studios (http://www.geniesoftstudios.com/), a software development company based in Melbourne, Victoria.

Steven is an experienced software developer with more than 13 years of experience in developing desktop and web-based applications for a number of companies, including insurance, banking and finance, oil and gas, and local and state government.

Steven is always interested in emerging technologies, and is a member of the SQL Server Special Interest Group (SQLSIG) and the Java Community. Steven has been the co-founder and Chief Technology Officer (CTO) of SoftMpire Pvt Ltd, a company that focused primarily on developing business applications for iOS and Android platforms.

He is also the author of *Xcode 4 iOS Development Beginner's Guide*.

You can check out his blog at http://geniesoftstudios.com/blog/, or follow him on Twitter at http://twitter.com/GenieSoftStudio.

Acknowledgements

No book is the product of just the author - he just happens to be the one with his name on the cover.

A number of people contributed to the success of this book, and it would take more space than I have to thank each one individually. A special shout, out goes to Steven Wilding, my acquisition editor, who is the reason that this book exists. Thank you, Steven, for believing in me, and for being a wonderful guide throughout this process. I would like to thank Alka Nayak for ensuring that I stayed on track and got my chapters in on time.

I would also like to thank both my development editors: Shreerang Deshpande and Maitreya Bhakal for their brilliant suggestions on how to improve the chapters, and to Lubna Shaikh for the fantastic job she has done, ensuring that we met the timeframes and delivery for this book.

Lastly, to my reviewers, thank you so much for your valued suggestions and improvements, making this book what it is. I am grateful to each and every one of you.

Thank you also to the entire Packt Publishing team for working so diligently to help bring out a high quality product. Finally, a big thank you to the engineers at Apple for creating the iPhone and the iPad, and for providing developers with the tools to create fun and sophisticated applications. You guys rock.

Finally, I'd like to thank all of my friends for their support, understanding, and encouragement during the writing process. It is a privilege to know each one of you.

About the Reviewers

Cory Bohon is an indie developer, creating iOS and Mac software using many programming languages, including Objective-C, Java, and C/C++. He is also a technology blogger on `http://www.maclife.com/`, where he writes about Apple news, and Mac and iOS how tos.

Chris Gummer graduated with a Bachelor's of Science majoring in Computing Science and Statistics, in Sydney, Australia. For over a decade, he has developed various software systems across a range of industries. Currently living in London, UK he specializes in iOS application development. He has worked on high profile App Store applications and internal enterprise solutions for iOS devices. At the age of eight, Chris started programming in BASIC, and he still holds the same passion for programming almost thirty years later.

Thanh Huynh started his career as a LAMP developer, with over 10 years experience, and gradually moved into objective-C. Currently working as a freelance iOS developer, he has worked for two of the biggest media companies in the United Kingdom, News International and BSkyB, producing the Times iPad app and Sky Plus.

Robb Lewis is a web developer and student studying web technologies at Portsmouth University. Robb has a great interest in technology, specifically mobile technology, and is an Apple advocate. Robb also writes about software, technology, and the internet at `http://therobb.com`.

Dan Lingman got his start in programming back in grade 7, when, after seeing a Space Invaders arcade game, he signed up for a night school course in programming the Commodore Pet. This eventually led to a M.Sc. in Computer Science, with his thesis project being a 3D robotics simulator programming in Objective-C on a NeXTStation.

By day, he works for a licensing company, and by night teaches Java development. He also works on iOS development as the technical lead at NoGoToGames.

NoGoToGames is a small company focused on the development of interesting and genre-breaking iOS software. You can see what they are up to at `http://www.nogotogames.com/`.

I'd like to thank my wife, May, and my daughters, Katrina and Naomi for their patience while I worked on reviewing this book.

www.PacktPub.com

Support files, eBooks, discount offers and more

You might want to visit www.PacktPub.com for support files and downloads related to your book.

Did you know that Packt offers eBook versions of every book published, with PDF and ePub files available? You can upgrade to the eBook version at www.PacktPub.com and as a print book customer, you are entitled to a discount on the eBook copy. Get in touch with us at service@packtpub.com for more details.

At www.PacktPub.com, you can also read a collection of free technical articles, sign up for a range of free newsletters and receive exclusive discounts and offers on Packt books and eBooks.

http://PacktLib.PacktPub.com

Do you need instant solutions to your IT questions? PacktLib is Packt's online digital book library. Here, you can access, read and search across Packt's entire library of books.

Why Subscribe?

- Fully searchable across every book published by Packt
- Copy and paste, print and bookmark content
- On demand and accessible via web browser

Free Access for Packt account holders

If you have an account with Packt at www.PacktPub.com, you can use this to access PacktLib today and view nine entirely free books. Simply use your login credentials for immediate access.

Instant Updates on New Packt Books

Get notified! Find out when new books are published by following @PacktEnterprise on Twitter, or the *Packt Enterprise* Facebook page.

This book is dedicated to:

My favorite uncle, Benjamin Jacob Daniel, for always making me smile, and for inspiring me to work hard and achieve my dreams. I miss you a lot.

Chan Ban Guan, for the continued patience, encouragement, support, and most of all, for believing in me during the writing of this book.

Mum and Dad, for always believing in me and for your continued love and support.

My sister Linda, thanks for always being there for me when I needed you most. I love you.

My brother Stuart, thanks for everything Bro.

My niece Ava Madison Daniel, thanks for bringing joy to our family. You're so cute.

This book would not have been possible without your love and understanding.

Lastly, to my dear friends. Thanks again for your continued love, support and understanding during the writing of this book. It really means a lot to me.

I would like to thank you from the bottom of my heart.

Table of Contents

Preface

Building on the phenomenal success of its predecessor, iOS 5 includes over 200 new user features as well as an updated SDK containing over 1,500 new APIs. iOS 5 looks set to reinforce the iPhone's dominance in the smartphone market.

iOS 5 Essentials will help you learn how to build simple, yet powerful iOS 5 applications, incorporating iCloud Storage, Twitter, Core Image and Newsstand integration.

You will start by learning about what's new in iOS 5. You'll look at the iCloud Storage APIs, Automatic Reference Counting, Twitter, and AirPlay integration, how to use the various Core Image filters using the Cocoa framework, and the new features of the iOS 5 SDK. After this, you'll jump straight in and create applications using Xcode and Interface Builder using the new storyboard layout. We then finish up by learning how to make your applications run smoothly using the Xcode instruments.

In this book, I have tried my best to keep the code simple and easy-to-understand. I have provided step-by-step instructions with loads of screenshots at each step to make it easier to follow. You will soon be mastering the different aspects of iOS 5 programming, as well as mastering the technology and skills needed to create some stunning applications. Feel free to contact me at geniesoftstudios@gmail.com for any queries, or just want to say 'hello'. Any suggestions for improving this book will be highly regarded.

What this book covers

Chapter 1, What's New in iOS5, introduces the developer to the Xcode developer set of tools, the new features of iOS 5, as well as an introduction into Newsstand and the `MessageUI` framework.

Chapter 2, Using iCloud and the Storage APIs, introduces you to the benefits of using iCloud, and how to incorporate iCloud functionality into your applications to store and retrieve files, and its data through the use of the storage APIs. This chapter will also give you some insight into how to go about handling file-version conflicts when multiple copies of the same file are being updated on more than one iOS device.

Chapter 3, Debugging with OpenGL ES, focuses on the differences between vertex shaders and fragment shaders, and their relationship with one another. We will become familiar with the OpenGL ES 2.0 Programmable pipeline, and look into the new debugging features of OpenGL ES that enables us to track down issues specific to OpenGL ES, right within the Xcode IDE. We will learn more about the OpenGL ES frame capture tool and its ability to stop execution of a program, that will enable the developer to grab the current frame contents that are being rendered on the iOS device, so that program issues can be tracked down and corrected, by taking a closer look at the program state information of objects, by scrolling through the debug navigator stack trace with the ability to see all of the textures and shaders that are currently being used by the application.

Chapter 4, Using Storyboards, gains an understanding of what Storyboards are and how we can apply the various transitions between views. We will take a look into how we are able to create and configure scenes and storyboard files, to present these programmatically. We will also look at how to go about building and integrating Twitter capabilities into our application to tweet photos and standard messages.

Chapter 5, Using AirPlay and Core Image, focuses on learning about the AirPlay and Core Image frameworks, and how we go about using and implementing these into our applications. This chapter also explains the different image filter effects, how to adjust the brightness of an image, as well as how to go about producing a water ripple effect. It also covers how to incorporate AirPlay functionality into your application, so that you can have your application displayed out to an external device, such as an Apple TV.

Chapter 6, Xcode Tools - Improvements, focuses on learning about the improvements that have been made to the Xcode development tools. We will take a look at **Automatic Reference Counting** (**ARC**), which is the latest addition that has been made to the LLVM compiler, and how this can help improve application performance, by minimizing issues with our applications. It also covers improvements that have been made to Interface Builder, the iOS Location simulator, and the set of debugging tools for OpenGL ES.

Chapter 7, Making your Applications Run Smoothly Using Instruments, focuses on how we can effectively use Instruments within our applications to track down memory leaks and bottlenecks within our applications that could potentially cause our application to crash on the user's iOS device. We will take a look into each of the different types of built-in instruments that come as part of the Instruments application, learn how we can use the System Trace instrument to monitor system calls, and track down performance issues within an application.

What you need for this book

This book assumes that you have an Intel-based Macintosh running Snow Leopard (Mac OS X 10.6.2, or later). You can use Leopard, but I would highly recommend upgrading to Snow Leopard or Lion, as there are many new features in Xcode that are available only to these two operating systems.

We will be using Xcode 4.2.1, which is the integrated development environment used for creating applications for iOS development. You can download the latest version of Xcode at the following link: `http://developer.apple.com/xcode/`.

Who this book is for

If you ever wanted to learn about the latest features of iOS 5 and learn how to incorporate Twitter, iCloud and Core Image framework effects functionality into your applications, then this book is for you. You should have a good knowledge of programming experience with Objective-C, and have used Xcode 4. iOS programming experience is not required.

Conventions

In this book, you will find a number of styles of text that distinguish between different kinds of information. Here are some examples of these styles, and an explanation of their meaning.

Code words in text are shown as follows: "Launch Xcode from the /Developer/ Applications folder."

A block of code is set as follows:

```
#import <UIKit/UIKit.h>
#import <MessageUI/MessageUI.h>

@interface MyEmailAppViewController:
  UIViewController<MFMailComposeViewControllerDelegate> {}
@end
```

When we wish to draw your attention to a particular part of a code block, the relevant lines or items are set in bold:

```
<plist version="1.0">
  <dict>
    <key>application-identifier</key>
    <string>AXEUZ3F6VR.com.geniesoftstudios</string>
    <key>com.apple.developer.ubiquity-container-identifiers</key>
    <array>
      <string>TEAMID.com.yourcompany.iCloudExample</string>
    </array>
    <key>com.apple.developer.ubiquity-kvstore-identifier</key>
    <string>TEAMID.com.yourcompany.iCloudExample</string>
    <key>get-task-allow</key>
    <true/>
  </dict>
</plist>
```

New terms and **important words** are shown in bold. Words that you see on the screen, in menus or dialog boxes for example, appear in the text like this: "When Xcode is launched, you should see the **Welcome to Xcode** screen."

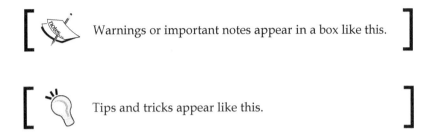

> Warnings or important notes appear in a box like this.

> Tips and tricks appear like this.

Feedback from our readers is always welcome. Let us know what you think about this book—what you liked or may have disliked. Reader feedback is important for us to develop titles that you really get the most out of.

To send us general feedback, simply send an e-mail to feedback@packtpub.com, and mention the book title through the subject of your message.

If there is a topic that you have expertise in and you are interested in either writing or contributing to a book, see our author guide on www.packtpub.com/authors.

Customer support

Now that you are the proud owner of a Packt book, we have a number of things to help you to get the most from your purchase.

Downloading the example code

You can download the example code files for all Packt books you have purchased from your account at http://www.packtpub.com. If you purchased this book elsewhere, you can visit http://www.packtpub.com/support and register to have the files e-mailed directly to you.

Errata

Although we have taken every care to ensure the accuracy of our content, mistakes do happen. If you find a mistake in one of our books—maybe a mistake in the text or the code—we would be grateful if you would report this to us. By doing so, you can save other readers from frustration and help us improve subsequent versions of this book. If you find any errata, please report them by visiting http://www.packtpub.com/support, selecting your book, clicking on the **errata submission form** link, and entering the details of your errata. Once your errata are verified, your submission will be accepted and the errata will be uploaded to our website, or added to any list of existing errata, under the Errata section of that title.

Piracy

Piracy of copyright material on the Internet is an ongoing problem across all media. At Packt, we take the protection of our copyright and licenses very seriously. If you come across any illegal copies of our works, in any form, on the Internet, please provide us with the location address or website name immediately so that we can pursue a remedy.

Please contact us at copyright@packtpub.com with a link to the suspected pirated material.

We appreciate your help in protecting our authors, and our ability to bring you valuable content.

Questions

You can contact us at questions@packtpub.com if you are having a problem with any aspect of the book, and we will do our best to address it.

1
What's New in iOS5

Welcome to the exciting world of iOS 5, the latest release of Apple's mobile operating system, which is packed with some great new features and improvements to the way things are done. The release of the iPhone 4, back in 2010, took the world by storm. Developers around the world have been embracing the new features, such as incorporating AirPlay features within their applications, making use of the retina display to provide crisp and high-definition graphics within their applications and games, as well as the accelerometer and gyroscope.

When Apple hosted their annual World Wide Developer Conference in June 2011, they introduced more than 200 new features, as well as an updated SDK that features over 1,500 new development APIs. This opened up a lot of ideas for many new applications and the way we do things currently, to be done differently. Some of the great new feature highlights are the ability to support the way in which notification messages are handled by using the new **Notification Center**, messaging has been greatly improved by using the new **iMessage** messaging application, and finally, the ability to organize and purchase all of your newspaper and magazine subscriptions using the new **Newsstand** application.

In this chapter, you will gain an insight into some of the fantastic new features and enhancements that have been incorporated into the latest iOS 5 release. We will also look at how to go about downloading and installing the Xcode developer tools and **Software Development Kit (SDK)**.

In this chapter, we will:

- Get introduced to some of the new features that come with iOS 5
- Download and install the Xcode development tools
- Create a simple application using the features of the Newsstand framework
- Create a simple application that sends an e-mail, using the `MessageUI` framework
- Remove the Xcode development tools

We have a exciting journey ahead of us, so let's get started.

What's new in iOS 5

Since the release of Apples iOS operating system back in June 2007, they have incorporated many new features and improvements within each release build of its operating system. In iOS 4, we saw this came with over 1,500 new APIs, as well as some high quality enhancements and improvements.

In iOS 5, Apple has introduced over 200 new features and improvements, as well as 1,500 new APIs and updates to its SDK, to include new features relating to Core Image, Twitter integration, and the Newsstand Kit.

Needless to say, the Xcode 4 development environment has also undergone some improvements to allow your applications to be compiled with the new LLVM compiler 3.0 that supports **Automatic Reference Counting** (**ARC**). Hence, you rarely need to retain or release your objects, as ARC does most of the work for you. In some cases, you will still need to use retain/release. Storyboard support has also been integrated into Interface Builder, which allows you to design multiple-view workflows for each of your views.

Lastly, debugging OpenGL ES projects are a lot easier, as these have been integrated into the Xcode debugging interface.

In the following sections, we will focus in detail on some of the new features that come with iOS 5.

Reminders

A neat new feature that comes as part of this release is the **Reminders App**. A good way to think of reminders would be to think of them as to-do lists. Reminders can prove to be a life-saver, as they give you the flexibility to organize your day-to-day tasks, and come complete with the ability to add due dates and locations.

When you set up your reminders to use locations, you can specify to be reminded on a specific day or location, as well as being reminded either when you arrive or leave the location. They make use of your mobile phone's GPS, similar to how your car's navigation system works, and are designed to alert you as soon as you approach the designated area. Let's take an example, say for instance, you wanted to buy a new printer and some additional ink, you set up your reminder to automatically send you an alert as soon as you pulled into your local stores, parking lot.

Finally, another thing to mention about reminders: since these have been integrated into iOS 5, they have been designed to work well with other applications. For example, Apple iCal, Microsoft Outlook, and iCloud. This has been done to ensure that any changes you make will automatically update on all of your devices and calendars.

The following screenshots shows a list of items that have been added to a to-do list, and then shows how you can configure and specify when to be reminded. You can choose to be reminded when you leave or arrive at a particular location. The final screenshot shows the reminder pop-up when the specified time has been reached. Additional items can be added to the list by selecting the **+** plus sign, as highlighted by a rectangle.

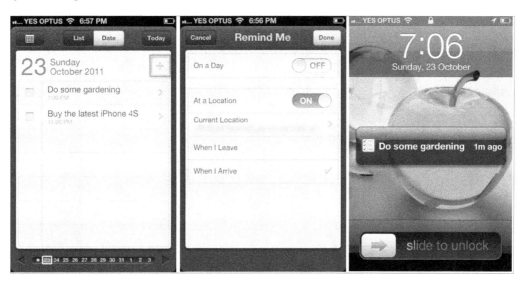

Notification Center

Notifications play an important role in an iPhone user's everyday life. Notifications come in the form of pop-ups to inform you that a new e-mail has arrived, of new SMS text messages, of friend requests from social networking sites, notifications when your phone credit falls below a certain amount, and much more. With the Notification Center application, you don't need to worry about locating that e-mail, SMS text message, or friend request. It has been made simple enough for you to keep track of all of these forms of notifications in one convenient location.

The Notification Center can be accessed by simply placing your finger anywhere at the top of the screen and swiping in a downward motion. There are many different notifications to choose from when you are in this view. For instance, you can choose to see the current weather forecast, your stock shares, calendar entries of upcoming appointments, and so on. As new notifications come through, they will be added and will appear at the top of the list for easier access, without interrupting what you're doing.

You can also act upon Notifications through the **lock** screen on your iOS device; these appear categorized within a table view, so that you can act on them quickly by simply sliding the panel to unlock and take you to the relevant application. For example, if you receive a message, this will open up the **iMessage** application. As you can see, the Notification Center provides you with a much better way of staying on top of your life's activities.

Newsstand

The **Newsstand** is a central place, where iOS users can access their subscribed magazines and newspapers. Unlike iBooks, where book publishers supply .epub files or similar documents, Newsstand publishers will have to create an iOS application (or adapt their existing application). Think of it like a cross between the shelf seen in the iBooks application and applications folders on the home screen.

To make use of the new features, publishers must invoke the newly added **Newsstand Kit framework**. There are some simple settings that need to be configured to allow your application to recognize that it is a magazine or a newspaper, so that it can be placed within the Newsstand application, instead of running as a standalone application.

In the coming section, we will proceed to download and install the iOS 5 SDK. If you have already installed this, you can skip this section altogether and proceed to the next section.

Getting and installing the iOS 5 SDK

Before we can start to build our iOS applications, you must first sign up as a registered iOS Developer at http://developer.apple.com/programs/ios/. The registration process is free and provides you with access to the iOS SDK and other developer resources that are really useful for getting you started.

Once you have signed up, you can then download the iOS SDK, as shown in the following screenshot. It may be worthwhile making sure that your machine satisfies the following system requirements prior to your downloading the iOS SDK:

- Only Intel Macs are supported, so if you have another processor type (such as the older G4 or G5 Macs), you're out of luck
- You have updated your system with the latest Mac OS X software updates for either OS X Lion or Snow Leopard

If you want to develop applications for the iPad and iPod Touch, you can still use the iOS SDK, as they use the same **operating system (OS)** as the iPhone does. This SDK allows you to create universal applications that will work with both the iPhone and iPad running on iOS 4 and above.

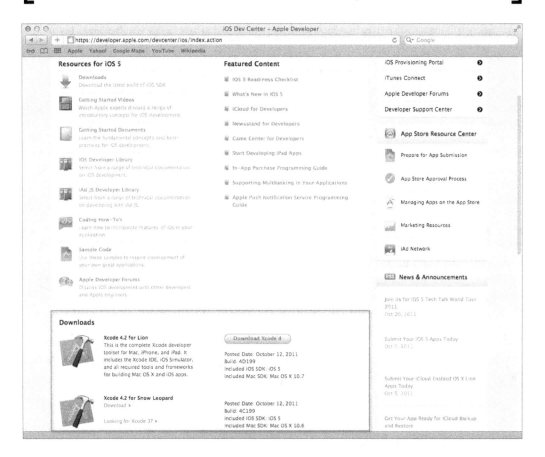

Once you have downloaded the SDK, you can proceed with installing it. You will be required to accept a few licensing agreements. You will then be presented with a screen to specify the destination folder in which to install the SDK:

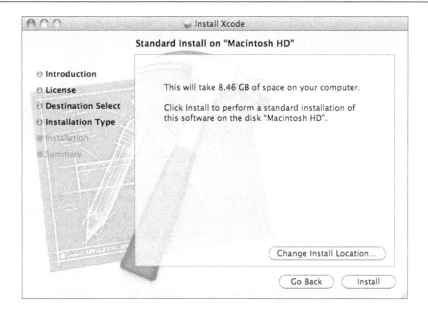

If you select the default settings during the installation phase, the various tools (explained in detail later) will be installed in the /Developer/Applications folder.

The installation process takes you through the custom installation option screens. You probably would have seen similar screens to this if you have installed other Mac software. The following screenshot shows what you will see here:

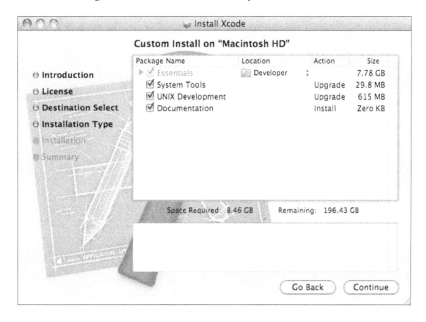

These options give you a little more control over the installation process. For example, you are able to specify the folder location to install Xcode, as well as settings for a variety of other options.

The iOS 5 SDK comes as part of the Xcode Developer Tools download, which you'll find at `https://developer.apple.com/devcenter/ios/index.action`.

The SDK consists of the following components:

- **Xcode**: This is the main **Integrated Development Environment** (**IDE**) that enables you to manage, edit, and debug your projects

- **Dashcode**: This enables you to develop web-based iOS applications and Dashboard widgets

- **iOS Simulator**: This is a Cocoa-based application that provides a software simulator to simulate an iOS device on your Mac OS X

- **Instruments**: These are the analysis tools that help you optimize your applications and monitor for memory leaks in real-time

The following screenshot displays a list of the various tools that are installed as part of the default settings, during the installation phase. These are installed in the `/Developer/Applications` folder:

In the next section, we will look at how we can use the power of the Newsstand Kit framework to enable developers to develop an application that will add items to our Newsstand, rather than this being launched as a separate iOS application.

Creating the MyMagazineArticle application

Before we can proceed with creating our MyMagazineArticle application, we must first launch the Xcode4.2 development environment. Double-click on the Xcode icon located in the /Developer/Applications folder.

Alternatively, you can use Spotlight to search for this: simply type Xcode into the search box and Xcode should be displayed in the list at the top. When Xcode is launched, you should see the **Welcome to Xcode** screen, as shown in the following screenshot.

It may be worth docking the Xcode icon to your Mac OS X launch bar for easy access, as we will be using it a lot throughout this book.

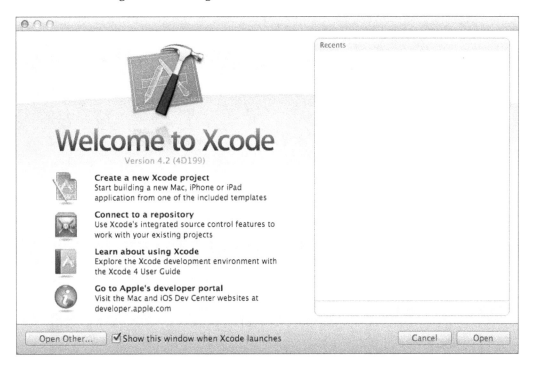

It is very simple to create the MyMagazineArticle application in Xcode. Just follow the steps listed here:

1. Select **Create a new Xcode project**, then select **iOS Application** on the left.

2. Select the **Page-Based Application** template from the **Project** template dialog-box.

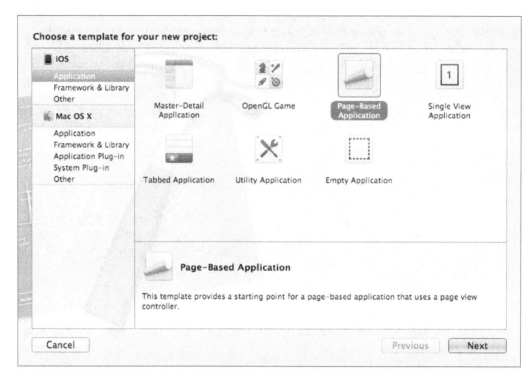

3. Then, click on the **Next** button to proceed to the next step in the wizard. This will allow you to enter in the **Product Name** and your **Company Identifier**.

 The company identifier for your App needs to be unique. Apple recommends that you use the reverse-domain style (for example, com.DomainName.AppName).

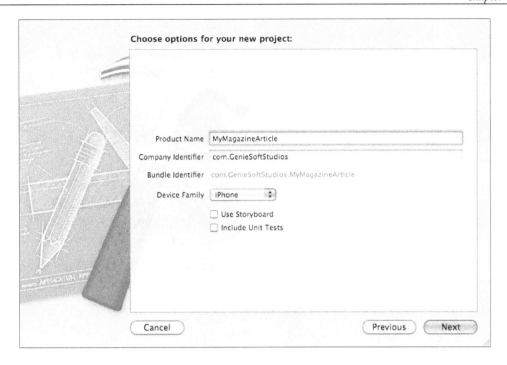

4. Enter in `MyMagazineArticle` for the **Product Name**, and enter a unique identifier in the **Company Identifier** field, ensuring that you have selected **iPhone** from the **Device Family** drop-down box.

5. Then, click on the **Next** button to proceed to the final step in the wizard.

6. Choose the folder location where you would like to save your project.

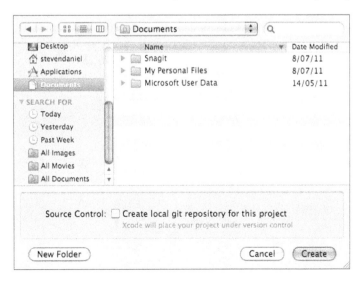

7. Then, click on the **Create** button to save your project at the location specified.

Once your project has been created, you will be presented with the Xcode development interface, along with the project files that the template created for you, within the **Project Navigator** window.

Adding the Newsstand Kit framework to our project

Now that we have created our project, we need to add the Newsstand Kit framework to our project. This is an important framework that provides us with the ability to make our application appear within the Newsstand application, provided in the latest iOS 5release.

To add this framework and any other frameworks to your project, select the **Project Navigator Group**, and then follow the simple steps outlined here:

1. Select your project within the **Project Navigator Window**.
2. Select your project target from under the **TARGETS** group.
3. Select the **Build Phases** tab.
4. Expand the **Link Binary with Libraries** disclosure triangle.
5. Scroll down within the list and select the **NewsstandKit.framework**, and click on the **Add** button to add the item to our project. You can use the **+** button to add the library that you want to add; to remove a framework, highlight it from the group, and then click on the **-** button. There is also the ability to search for the framework, if you can't find it in the list shown.
6. If you are still confused on how to go about adding the NewsstandKit. framework, you can refer to the following screenshot, which highlights what parts you need to select (highlighted by a rectangle).

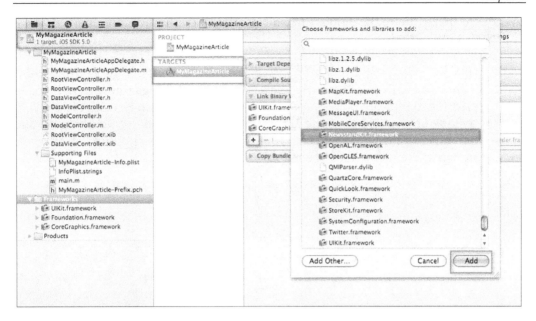

Adding properties to our application

Now that we have added the `NewsstandKit.framework` to our project, our next step is to start adding some properties to make our application show up within the Newsstand application.

Unlike other iOS applications, Newsstand applications that you create will only appear in the Newsstand application, and not displayed within the user's home screen like iOS applications currently do. Instead of displaying the application icon, the application will display a cover and some additional information provided by Newsstand. When a user taps the cover of your application, it will automatically launch your application and present them with information pertaining to that article.

Creating an application that uses the Newsstand Kit requires communication between your application and the servers that host your content. Your servers are responsible for notifying the application when any new updates or releases are available, typically using a **push** notification.

For more information on push notifications, refer to the Apple Developer Connection documentation which can be found at the following address: http://developer.apple.com/library/ios/#documentation/ NetworkingInternet/Conceptual/RemoteNotificationsPG/ Introduction/Introduction.html.

In order to make our application act like a Newsstand application, and make it appear on the shelf, three steps are required. These are:

1. Add the Newsstand Kit framework to your project.

2. Include the **UINewsstandApp** key within your **MyMagazineArticle-Info. plist** file to indicate that it supports Newsstand. This can be achieved by clicking on the **MyMagazineArticle-Info.plist** file, then right-clicking within the center of the panel, and selecting **Add Row** from the pop-up list, as shown in the following screenshot:

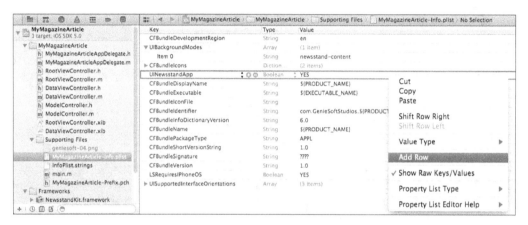

3. Include the **Required background modes** key with the newsstand-content value, for the application to be launched in the background so that it can start downloading the latest content. This can be achieved by clicking on the MyMagazineArticle-Info.plist file, and then right-clicking within the center of the panel and selecting Add Row from the pop-up list.

The following screenshot shows the options that are needed to be assigned to, make it appear within the Newsstand folder:

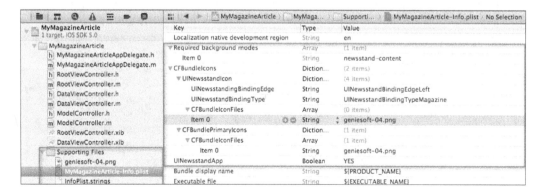

If your Newsstand application includes the required background modes key within the **newsstand-content** value, located within the **MyMagazineArticle-Info.plist** file, your newsstand application will be launched in the background, so that it can start downloading the latest version of your magazine or newspaper article.

The download process is self-managed, and is taken care of by the system, which then notifies your application when the content has been fully downloaded and made available.

In order to make our application appear within the newsstand folder, you will need to create an array entry **CFBundleIconFiles** under the **CFBundlePrimaryIcons** to include your standard application icon.

You then need to create your **UINewsstandIcon** with a **CFBundle** in there as well, as this is where you set your newspaper or magazine covers and specify the binding type, which gives your application an icon shape and its binding edge.

In the following screenshot, it shows how we can customize our application to have it show as a newspaper, by changing the **UINewsstandBindingType** property to **UINewsstandBindingTypeNewspaper**:

CFBundleIcons	Diction...	(2 items)
▼ UINewsstandIcon	Diction...	(4 items)
UINewsstandingBindingEdge	String	UINewsstandBindingEdgeLeft
UINewsstandBindingType	String	UINewsstandBindingTypeNewspaper
▼ CFBundleIconFiles	Array	(0 items)
Item 0	String	geniesoft-04.png
▼ CFBundlePrimaryIcons	Diction...	(1 item)
▼ CFBundleIconFiles	Array	(1 item)
Item 0	String	geniesoft-04.png

Once you have created these entries within your application's .plist file, by making sure that you have added the actual icon .png files to your project, you will be ready to compile, build, and run your application. The following screenshot will be displayed, which shows that our application has been successfully added as part of the **Newsstand** folder application, with its icon changed to display as a newspaper article.

When adding icons to your project, it is important to take note of the size. This is dependent whether or not you are developing this for an iPhone or iPad. In the following table, this lists the name, size, and platform that the icons pertain to.

Image name	Size (pixels)	iOS Platform
Icon.png	57x57	Universal application icon
Icon-72.png	72x72	iPad
Icon-64.png	64x64	iPad
Icon-32.png	32x32	iPad/iPhone
Icon-24.png	24x24	iPad/iPhone
Icon-16.png	16x16	iPad/iPhone

If we change the **UINewsstandBindingType** property back to **UINewsstandBindingTypeMagazine**, it will display our icon as a magazine cover.

Once you have modified this entry within your application's `.plist` file, you will be ready to compile, build, and run this application. The following screenshot will be displayed, which shows that our application has successfully been added as part of the **Newsstand** folder application, with its icon changed to display as a **Magazine** cover.

So there you have it. As you can see, by adding some simple properties to your applications .plist file, you can customize your application to either have its icon displayed as a magazine cover, or as a newspaper article.

 One important thing to mention is that Newsstand applications must include the **UINewsstandApp** key within your project's .plist file, to indicate that it supports the Newsstand feature. If this is not done, your application will appear as a normal application that will be displayed on the user's home screen.

Creating the MyEmailApp application

Sending an e-mail from within your application ensures that you don't need to re-launch your application after sending the e-mail. This can be a good thing, as it makes your application user-friendly, enabling the user to keep using your application without having to re-launch it.

In this section, we will be using the MessageUI framework to create a simple application that will allow in-app sending of e-mails, without the user having to exit your application and then re-launch it.

We will also look at how we can automatically fill the **To**, **Subject**, and **Message Body** fields, before finally seeing how we can access and customize the navigation bar color to suit your application. To see how we can achieve this, just follow these simple steps:

1. Launch Xcode from the /Developer/Applications folder.
2. Then, choose the **Single View Application** template from the project template dialog box:

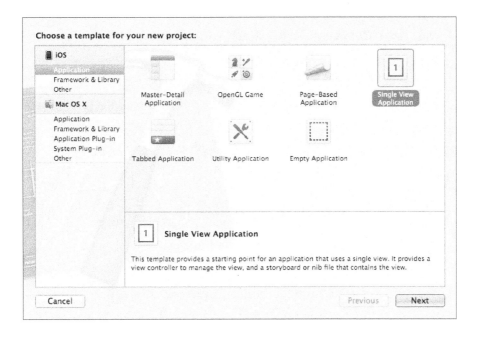

3. Click on the **Next** button to proceed to the next step within the wizard.

4. Provide a name for your project by filling in the **Product Name** and **Company Identifier** fields.

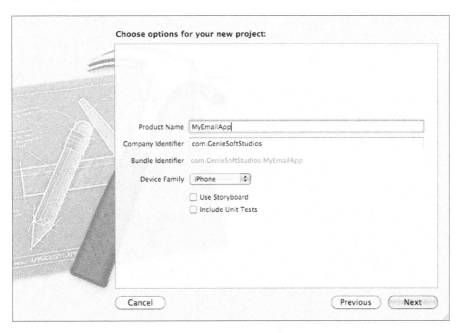

5. Enter in MyEmailApp for the **Product Name**.

6. Ensure that **iPhone** is selected from the **Device Family** drop-down box.

7. Click on **Next**, to proceed to the final step in the wizard.

8. Choose the folder location where you would like to save your project.

9. Then, click on the **Create** button to save your project at the location specified.

Adding the MessageUI framework to our project

Now that we have created our project, we need to add the MessageUI Framework to our project. This is an important framework that will provide us with the ability to send an e-mail message.

To add this framework, follow these simple steps:

1. Select your project within the **Project Navigator Window**.

2. Then, select your project target from under the **TARGETS** group.

3. Select the **Build Phases** tab.

4. Expand the **Link Libraries** with **Libraries** disclosure triangle.

5. Then, scroll down within the list and select the MessageUI.framework, and click on the **Add** button to add the item to our project. You can use the **+** button to add the library that you want to add; to remove a framework, highlight it from the group, and then click on the **–** button.

6. If you are still confused as to how to go about adding the **MessageUI. framework**, you can refer to the following image, which highlights what parts you need to select (highlighted by a rectangle).

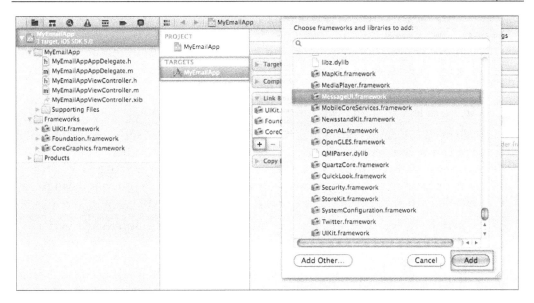

Building TheMyEmailApp user interface

In this section, we will start to build our user interface for the `MyEmailApp`. We will need to include the header file information for the `MessageUI` framework, which we added in the previous section.

This exposes all of the function methods and parameter calls. To see how this can be achieved, follow these simple steps:

1. Now that we have added the required framework, our next step is to import the framework header file into our `MyEmailAppViewController.h` header file as follows:

   ```
   #import <MessageUI/MessageUI.h>
   ```

2. Next, under the resources folder, open the `MyEmailAppViewController.xib` file, then drag a `UIButton` control from the **Object Library**, and set the buttons caption to display `Send Email` through its text property, or you can double-click on the button and type in the `Send Email` text.

   We need to create the method action event that will execute when this button has been pressed.

3. In the `MyEmailAppViewController.m` implementation file, add the following code:

   ```
   - (IBAction)composeEmail{
     MFMailComposeViewController *controller =
       [[MFMailComposeViewControlleralloc] init];
   ```

```
[selfpresentModalViewController:controlleranimated:YES];

controller.mailComposeDelegate = self [controller release];
}
```

This creates an `MFMailComposeViewController` object, and sets ourself up as the delegate, so that we can receive the callbacks.

4. We need to dismiss our e-mail window view once we have sent our message. For this to happen, we need to implement a delegate handler to our mail compose view controller `MFMailComposeViewControllerDelegate`. This sets up your applications view-controller as the delegate, so that it can be notified when the user either sends or cancels the e-mail.

5. Open the `MyEmailAppViewController.h` interface file, and then add the following code:

```
#import <UIKit/UIKit.h>
#import <MessageUI/MessageUI.h>

@interface MyEmailAppViewController:
    UIViewController<MFMailComposeViewControllerDelegate> {}
@end
```

6. We now need to implement a callback method, which will be used to dismiss the view controller when the user sends or cancels the e-mail.

7. Open the `MyEmailAppViewController.m` implementation file, and add the following code:

```
- (void)mailComposeController:(MFMailComposeViewController*)
  controller didFinishWithResult:(MFMailComposeResult)result
  error:(NSError*)error {
  [selfdismissModalViewControllerAnimated:YES];
}
```

Auto-populating fields

So far, we have added enough program logic to allow our application to function correctly, but this doesn't allow for certain fields to be auto-populated, so these will need to be manually filled in. To do this, we first need to add some additional code.

1. Open the `MyEmailAppViewController.m` implementation file, and add the following code to the `composeEmail` method, as shown below:

```
[controllersetSubject:@"Program Bug"];

[controllersetToRecipients:[NSArrayarrayWithObject:
    [NSStringstringWithString:@"YourEmail@companyname.com"]]];
[controllersetMessageBody:@"An application error has occurred
    within module XcodeFunctions.m" isHTML:NO];

[controller.navigationBarsetTintColor:[UIColorredColor]];
[selfpresentModalViewController:controlleranimated:YES];

controller.mailComposeDelegate = self;
[controller release];
```

2. There is also the option to change the color of the navigation bar that is located at the top of the e-mail window. To achieve this, we need to use the `setTintColor` method of the `navigationBar` control. You will need to add this to the `composeEmail` method, just before the line that reads `[self pres entModalViewController:controller:`

```
[controller.navigationBarsetTintColor:[UIColorredColor]];
[selfpresentModalViewController:controlleranimated:YES];
```

In this section, we have successfully added the code to pre-fill our e-mail composition sheet with default item details, and looked at how we can set the color of our navigation bar. In the next section, we will take a look at how to build and run our application.

Building and running the MyEmailApp application

Once you have implemented the previous code, it is time to compile, build, and run your application to see how it all works. The following screenshot below displays the MyEmailApp application running within the iOS simulator, with all of the fields populated:

So, there you have it. You have successfully built an application using the MessageUI framework that sends a new e-mail message. When you press the **Send Email** button, it displays the compose new e-mail view controller window directly within your application, with all fields pre-populated, and the navigation bar is colored appropriately. The action sheet that is shown in the last screenshot gets displayed when you press the **Cancel** button.

iMessage

iMessage is an integrated add-on to the existing Messages application that we have come to know and love. iMessage allows you to easily send text messages, photos, videos, or other content to an individual or a group of people on other iOS devices running iOS 5 over Wi-Fi or 3G.

These messages are also automatically pushed to all of your other iOS devices, thus making it easier to maintain one conversation across all devices. When sending messages using iMessage, your phone automatically checks to see if the phone number of the person that you are sending is running iOS 5, if this is the case, it will send them an iMessage message rather than a standard SMS text.

Up to this point, your address book will be updated and a small blue chat bubble will appear next to the name of the contact to indicate that they can receive iMessages. If the person is not running iOS 5, then the address book will be updated with a green chat bubble. In the following screenshot, it displays the iMessages feature, and displays the conversations in small blue bubbles to indicate that both people are running iOS 5:

The bullet points below summarize some of the advantages of using iMessage, as opposed to the standard messaging component.

- iMessage brings the Message application for all iOS devices running iOS 5 – the iPhone, iPod touch, and iPad. Messages are pushed to all your devices, so if you start a conversion on your iPhone, you are able to continue and pick it upon any iOS device

- iMessage service is built into the Message application, so users can send unlimited text, photos, videos, contacts, locations, and group messages for free, to their family and friends who have an iOS device. It is worth mentioning that, while this feature doesn't incur any text messaging fees, it does use your bandwidth allocation, and depending on how much you use, it might cost you more.

- iMessage easily allows you to find out if someone is responding to your message in the form of an ellipsis, as seen on applications such as an instant messenger.

- iMessage optionally allows you to track your messages with delivery receipt and read receipt.

- You can send messages over Wi-Fi as well as over 3G.

- Messages that are sent through iMessage are encrypted over the air.

iPhone Camera

Another component within the iPhone that has been updated in this latest release, is the **iPhone Camera**. Since the camera is the most widely used application to capture those special and unexpected moments, Apple has made this more accessible.

This application can now be accessed directly from your iPhone's lock screen, and features several improvements, such as:

- **Grid lines**: These are very helpful for determining if the camera is leveled to ensure that you take a perfect shot every time, by using things in the horizon or edges of buildings.

- **Pinch-to-zoom gestures**: This feature enables you to manually zoom in and out, directly, within the camera application, rather than using the slider at the bottom of the screen.

- **Single-tap focus**: This feature allows you to lock the focus and the exposure to one area of the screen. Simply tap your finger anywhere on the screen.

- **Exposure locks to compose a picture on the fly**: This feature allows you to lock the focus and the exposure of your image, by simply placing and holding your finger on the screen.

There have also been new photo editing improvements added to the **Photos** application, to enable you to manipulate your images, to either crop or rotate your image, or provide photo enhancements, such as removal of red-eye from your photos, all done directly within the Photos application

If you are using iCloud (we will be covering this in *Chapter 2, Using iCloud and the Storage APIs*), it is also possible to automatically load new photos onto your computer's desktop, should you prefer to edit them there using your preferred photo-editing tool.

Access from Lock screen
Open the Camera app with one tap.

PC Free

With the new **PC Free** feature that comes with iOS 5, users can set up and activate their devices without the need of a computer. Any new iOS software updates are deployed directly to your iOS devices, as well as any purchases made on your device from iTunes or the App Store. These are transferred securely over Wi-Fi using **Secure Sockets Layer** (**SSL**) back to your iTunes library.

Once you have properly set up and configured iCloud, your backups and restores will automatically be done for you, and stored within the Cloud, making it easier for you to deploy any iOS updates to each of your iOS devices or computers that use the same Apple ID.

The following screenshot displays options on how to set up your phone, restore your device from and iCloud backup, or from your iTunes library. Once this is done, you will receive a final **Thank You** screen, where you can start using your iOS device.

Wi-Fi sync

In iOS 5, Apple has provided an easier way for its users to wirelessly synchronize all of your iOS devices over a shared Wi-Fi connection directly back to your Mac or PC, without the need of having it connected directly to your computer, as you would have done previously.

What happens is that, each time you decide to charge your iOS device, it will automatically search for any new purchases or items that have been added to your device and then automatically synchronize this back to your iTunes library.

In this manner, you will always have a back up copy of all of your movies, precious home videos, and photo albums in one place, which can be accessed anytime you want them.

Multitasking gestures

Unfortunately, these never made it in the iOS 4 release; they were only included in the iOS 4 SDK for developers, but ended-up working really well on the iPad. In iOS 5, this has been greatly improved and includes a number of added features to make accessing content a lot easier. The engineers at Apple have made it simpler, and a lot easier to navigate around in as little moves as possible. They have also added shortcut menus to help you get around even quicker on the iPad.

These are achieved by using four or five fingers, and swiping upwards to reveal the multitasking bar and using the pinch motion to return to the **Home** screen. There has even been support added relating to swiping left or right, to switch between your applications.

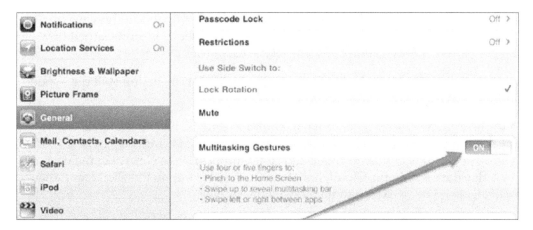

Removing the Xcode developer tools

Should you ever wish to uninstall Xcode (in the event that something went wrong during installation, or you just want to uninstall the Xcode developer tools), it is a very straightforward process. Open an instance of the terminal window and run the `uninstall-devtools` script:

```
sudo <Xcode>/Library/uninstall-devtools --mode=all
```

`<Xcode>` is the directory where the tools are installed. For typical installations, the full path is `/Developer/Library/uninstall-devtools`.

<sudo> is a system admin command that will require you to enter in the administrator password before proceeding.

 Before you proceed, make sure this is what you really intend to do, as once it's gone, it's permanently deleted. In any event, you can always choose to reinstall the Xcode developer tools. It is worth checking that the /Developer/Library/Xcode/ folder has also been removed. If not, just move it to the trash.

Summary

In this chapter, we learned about the new features of iOS 5, and how to go about downloading and installing the iOS 5 SDK, as well as familiarizing ourselves with some of the Xcode development tools.

We then moved on, and looked at how to build a simple Newsstand application, using the Newsstand Kit framework, to show how we can add newspapers and magazines to the Newsstand application folder. Next, we looked at how we can use the MessageUI framework to build a simple e-mail application, and learned how we can customize the navigation bar UI to set the background color.

To end the chapter, we looked at the steps involved on how to uninstall the Xcode developer tools, using the command line.

In the next chapter, we will learn what **iCloud** exactly is that we keep hearing so much about it, and we will focus on the storage APIs that comes as part of iCloud. We will take a look at how to create an iCloud application to store documents and key-value data within the Cloud, how to perform a backup to the Cloud, and then finally look at how we can handle file-version conflicts.

2
Using iCloud and the Storage APIs

In this chapter, we will be introducing the features of iCloud and their storage APIs. These allow you to develop your application to write and store user documents in a common and central location, with the ability to access those items from all of your computers and iOS devices.

Making a user's document available using iCloud, means that a user can view or edit those documents directly from any device, without the need of having to sync or transfer those files. Storing documents in a user's iCloud account provides an added layer of security for that user. Even if the user loses their device, the documents can easily be retrieved from the device, provided that they are contained within iCloud storage.

Through the use of the iCloud storage APIs, you can make your applications capable enough to store user documents and key-value data, allowing this information, and any changes to it, to be pushed to all of your iOS devices all at the same time. By using iCloud, you can create some excellent applications, by adding some great compelling functionality.

In this chapter, we will:

- Take advantage of iCloud storage
- Back up our data using iCloud backup
- Store documents within iCloud storage
- Search for documents within the Cloud
- Handle file-version conflicts
- Move and store documents to iCloud storage
- Configure and set up provisioning profiles ready for iCloud storage.

Let's get started.

Comparing Apple iCloud and Google Docs

When Apple announced their new cloud-based file management system called iCloud, it allowed you to backup your files to the Cloud, and synchronize your data between multiple devices.

Devices, such as the iPad and iPhone, can automatically backup files, such as photos, music, and documents to iCloud, and have these synchronize with your other Apple devices.

One of the significant differences you will notice between iCloud and Google Docs, is that, iCloud is meant only for Apple devices, such as the iPhone, iPod Touch and iPad.

iCloud works by storing all of your music, photos, documents, books, and so on, and automatically pushing them out to all of your other devices, wirelessly.

Any documents that are stored within iCloud can be accessed and viewed from any device that is connected to the Internet. At this stage, iCloud does not offer a way to share the documents with other users.

On the other hand, Google Docs is a free document management service from Google that allows you to create, edit, and manage various types of documents in the Cloud. This is all handled within an easy-to-use interface to manage your documents, each organized under labels that are equivalent to folders. Unlike iCloud, you are able to access these documents within the Cloud from any computer, tablet, or even using your iPhone and iPad.

Google Docs currently supports and stores the following file types within the Cloud. These can be later accessed from anywhere on the web.

- Documents
- Spreadsheets
- Presentations
- **Drawings**: This is a new addition to the Google Docs family.

iCloud and Google Docs both offer free storage, but come with some limitations. iCloud comes with a total limit of 5GB per account; additional space can be purchased should you require it.

Google Docs is also free, but comes with restrictions and limitations, based on the total number of documents that you can store and the length/content of each document.

Unlike iCloud, Google Docs provides you with a way of sharing your documents with other users.

You have the flexibility of sharing and setting user rights to your documents. You have the ability to make a document publicly available on the Internet with view only access, or allow selected people to edit.

Storing and using documents in iCloud

Storing documents within the Cloud provides you with a common central location for easy access to those documents. Any updates that are made to the document can then be delivered to every iOS device or computer, as long as they are using the same Apple ID used to upload those documents.

When a document is uploaded to iCloud, it is not moved there immediately. The document must first be moved out of the application sandbox into a local system-managed directory, where it can be monitored by the iCloud service.

Once this process has completed, the file is transferred to iCloud and then distributed out to the user's other iOS devices as soon as possible. While the files are stored within iCloud storage, any changes that are made on one device are initially stored locally and then immediately pushed out to iCloud, using a local daemon service.

This is to prevent file conflicts from happening at the same time; this is handled by the **File** coordinator, which mediates changes made between the application and the local daemon service that is responsible for facilitating the transfer of the document to-and-from the iCloud service.

The file coordinator acts much like a locking mechanism for the document, thus preventing your application and the daemon service from applying modifications to the document simultaneously.

Whenever your application stores documents to iCloud, it must specify one or more containers in which those documents, contents will be stored, by including the key value entry `com.apple.developer.ubiquity-container-identifiers` within your applications, entitlements file. This is covered in the section *Requesting entitlements for iCloud storage*.

The following screenshot shows the process when changes are made on one device, and having those changes stored locally before being pushed back out to the iCloud service using a local daemon process.

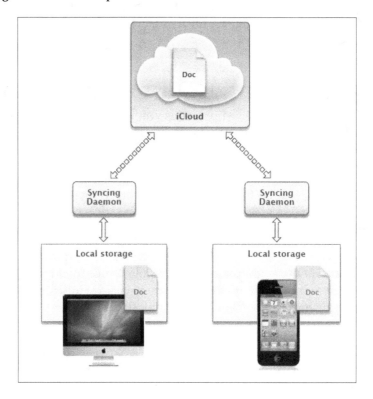

From an implementation perspective, the easiest way to provide your applications with the ability to manage documents stored within iCloud, would be to use the UIDocument class. This class handles everything that is required to read and write files that are stored within iCloud. It can:

- Handle the creation and use of the file coordinators to modify the document
- Seamlessly detect changes that are received from other devices
- Handle any potential conflicts that arise when two devices manage to update the same file in conflicting ways
- Prevent large number of conflicting changes from occurring at the same time

We will take a look at storing documents within iCloud, when we start to create our example application in our section on *Creating an iCloudExample Application*.

Storing key-value data in iCloud

Storing data within iCloud provides you with a means of making your applications share data between other copies of the same data running on other computers and other iOS devices.

The class that allows you to do this is called the NSUbiquitousKeyValueStore. This class provides you with the ability to share small amounts of data between your devices.

The NSUserDefaults class, provides you with a programmatic interface for interacting with the system defaults that allows an application to customize its behavior to match a user's preferences. For example, you can set up your application to specify how often documents are automatically saved. This class allows you to save your details to a variety of data types, that is, numbers, strings, dates, arrays and so on, before retrieving the data for use at a later time.

The main difference between the NSUserDefaults and the NSUbiquitousKeyValueStore, is that the NSUserDefaults class writes the data to the user's iCloud storage, so that it can be retrieved by the application running on a different iOS device or computer.

The following code snippet shows how to set up the cloud, so that you are able to write the data to the user's iCloud storage:

```
// TeamID + Bundle Identifier
NSFileManager *fileManager = [NSFileManagerdefaultManager];
NSURL *CloudURL = [fileManager URLForUbiquityContainerIdentifier:
  @"TEAMID.com.yourcompany.iCloudExample"];

// Log our iCloud URL to the console window
NSLog(@"iCloudURL: %@", [CloudURLabsoluteString]);

// Get a reference to the user's cloud store.
NSUbiquitousKeyValueStore *cloudStore =
  [NSUbiquitousKeyValueStoredefaultStore];

// Store our Cloud URL to the iCloudURL key.
[cloudStoresetString:[CloudURLabsoluteString] forKey:@"CloudURL"];

// This is important to include as it stores the
// values you set earlier on iCloud.
[cloudStore synchronize];
```

When using the `NSUbiquitousKeyValueStore` class, you must ensure that an entry to the `com.apple.developer.ubiquity-kvstore-identifier` entitlement is added to your project entitlements file. This is covered in the section *Requesting entitlements for iCloud storage*.

The amount of space available for a single key-value store is limited to 64KB; any data that is written to a single key-value within your container must not exceed 4KB in size. This is so that you can store small amounts of data about your application, but it is not advisable to use it to store user documents or large amounts of data.

For example, you may have an application that might store the current version number, and the name of the screen or document that the user was viewing. That way, if the user opens the application on another device, the version of your application on that device can open the same screen or document as the previous device.

Requesting entitlements for iCloud storage

In order to protect the data your application creates, a number of specific entitlements need to be created at build-time in order to use iCloud storage. You will need to ensure that you have selected the option to enable iCloud for your application's App ID.

You will need to either create a new App ID from within the iOS provisioning portal located at `https://developer.apple.com/devcenter/ios/index.action#`. Or, if you are using an existing ID, this must not be a wildcard one, that is, `com.yourcompany.*`.

To enable iCloud services for your App ID, follow these simple steps:

1. First, set up your provisioning profile for use with iCloud, by simply checking the **Enable for iCloud** checkbox from the **Configure App ID** screen.

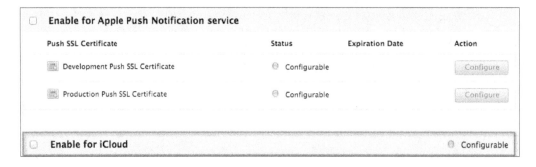

2. Next, you will be presented with a pop-up dialog box, explaining that any new provisioning profiles that you create using the chosen App ID will be enabled for iCloud services.

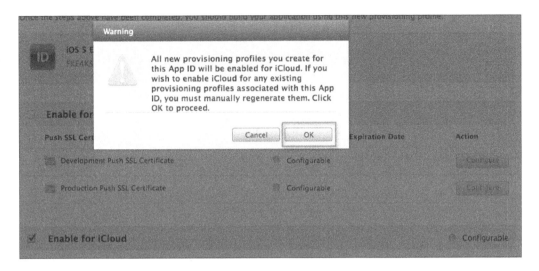

3. Once you have clicked on the **OK** button, the pop-up dialog box will disappear, and you will be returned back to the **Configure App ID** screen, and the **Enable for iCloud Enabled** button will be set to green, as shown in the following screenshot:

4. Click on the **Done** button to close this screen.

5. Next, from the **Provisioning** tab, download your **Development and Distribution Provisioning Profiles**.

6. Next, from the **ProjectNavigator** window, click on your project, then click on the **Targets** section, and then on the **Summary** page.

7. Scroll down till you get to the **Entitlements** section, and check the **Enable Entitlements** checkbox. This will add a file called **iCloudExample. entitlements** to your project.

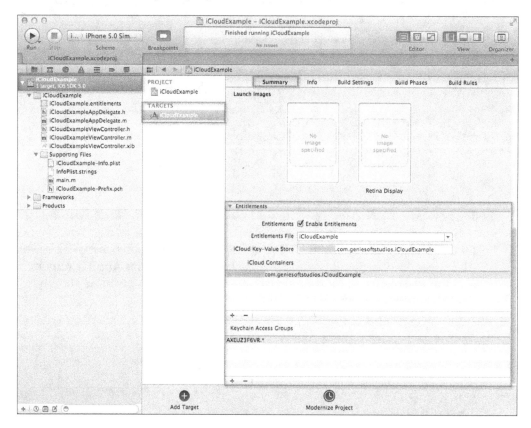

When you add entitlements to your project, they are bound directly to your applications provisioning profile that are used to separate your application's documents and data repositories from that of other applications that you create. There are two entitlements that an application can request, depending on which iCloud features it is required to use. These are explained in the following table.

Entitlement	Description
com.apple.developer.ubiquity-container-identifiers	Use this to request the iCloud document storage entitlement.
	The value of this key is an array of container-identifier strings (the first string in the array must not contain any wildcard characters).
com.apple.developer.ubiquity-kvstore-identifier	Use this to request the iCloud key-value data store entitlement. The value of this key is a single container identifier string.

When you specify the container identifier string, this must be in the form `<TEAMID>.<CUSTOM_STRING>`, where `<TEAMID>` is the unique ten-character identifier associated with your development team. The `<CUSTOM_STRING>` identifier is a reverse-DNS string that identifies the container for storing your application's documents.

This string does not necessarily need to be your application's bundle identifier, but can be anything that makes sense to you, or your development team.

 To locate your unique identifier associated with your development team, log in to the Apple developer connection website, and then go to the **Member Center** page (`http://developer.apple.com/membercenter`). From the **Member Center** home page, select the **Your Account** tab, and then select **Organization Profile** from the column on the left of that tab. Your team's identifier is in the **Company/Organization ID** field.

Applications using iCloud document storage can specify multiple containers for storing documents and data. The value of the `com.apple.developer.ubiquity-container-identifiers` key is an array of strings. The first string in this array must be the main container identifier to associate with your application.

The following code snippet shows the XML from the iCloudExample entitlements file that requests the keys for an iPhone application. It can read and write its own documents, which are stored in the container directory, identified as shown in the highlighted code sections.

```
<?xml version="1.0" encoding="UTF-8"?>
<!DOCTYPE plist PUBLIC "-//Apple//DTD PLIST 1.0//EN" "http://www.
apple.com/DTDs/PropertyList-1.0.dtd">
<plist version="1.0">
  <dict>
    <key>application-identifier</key>
    <string>AXEUZ3F6VR.com.geniesoftstudios</string>
    <key>com.apple.developer.ubiquity-container-identifiers</key>
    <array>
      <string>TEAMID.com.yourcompany.iCloudExample</string>
    </array>
    <key>com.apple.developer.ubiquity-kvstore-identifier</key>
    <string>TEAMID.com.yourcompany.iCloudExample</string>
    <key>get-task-allow</key>
    <true/>
  </dict>
</plist>
```

The following screenshot displays the property list view within the project navigator of the iCloudExample.Entitlements entitlements file.

Key	Type	Value
application-identifier	String	AXEUZ3F6VR.com.yourcompany
▼ com.apple.developer.ubiquity-container-	Array	(1 item)
Item 0	String	TEAMID.com.yourcompany.iCloudExample
com.apple.developer.ubiquity-kvstore-	String	TEAMID.com.yourcompany.iCloudExample
get-task-allow	Boolean	YES
▶ keychain-access-groups	Array	(1 item)

The **TEAMID** value (as shown in the previous screenshot), can be obtained from the **Account Summary** page of your **Developer Account** and using the **Individual ID**, as shown in the following screenshot:

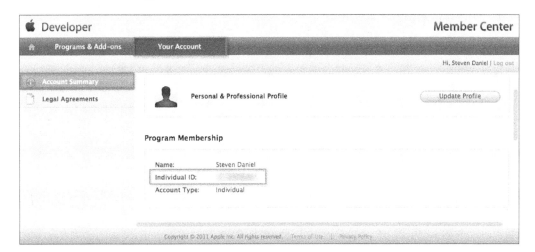

 The strings you specify in your entitlements property-list file are also the strings you pass to the URLForUbiquityContainerIdentifier: method, when requesting the location of a directory in the user's iCloud storage.

iCloud backup

When using backups with iCloud, users have the ability to choose to have their applications and data backed up directly to their iCloud account. This makes it easier to restore applications to their most recent state at a later time. Choosing to have data backed up to iCloud, will make it easier for a user to reinstall their data to any new or existing iOS device.

iCloud determines what files get backed up, and is based on the location where these files are kept, normally within the applications, home directory. Other areas that are backed up would be everything contained within the user's documents directory, as well as the contents of your applications library. When developing iCloud applications, and minimizing the amount of data stored in the user's iCloud account, you are encouraged to put more files in the Library/Caches directory, especially if those files can be easily re-created or obtained in another way.

In order to have your data backed-up to iCloud, you will need to activate this on all of your iOS devices. This can be achieved by following these simple steps:

1. From the **Settings** pane within your device, select **iCloud**. This is shown in the following screenshot:

2. Next, sign-in with your **AppleID** and **Password**, and then click on the **Sign In** button as shown in this screenshot.

3. You will need to agree to the iCloud terms and conditions, and then click on the **Agree** button to close the pop up dialog box.

4. In the next screenshot, you have the option to decide which items you would like to backup to iCloud.

5. Next, click on the **Storage & Backup** option to proceed to the next screen:

6. Next, set the **Back Up to iCloud** option to **ON**, from under the **Backup**
    sections pane. This will automatically backup all of your camera photos,
    documents, and settings to iCloud.

> Setting this option to **ON** will prevent iTunes from backing up your
> details, as your iOS device will handle this.

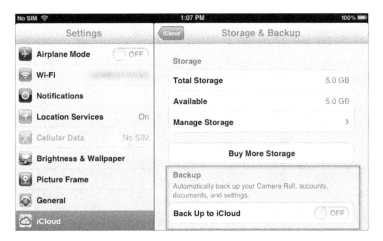

When using the iCloud storage APIs from within your applications, any documents that your application stores explicitly in iCloud are not backed up with your application; this is because these will already be stored within your iCloud account, and therefore do not need to be backed up separately.

For information on how to store documents within iCloud, refer to the section *Storing and using documents in iCloud*. To determine which directories are backed up, check out the **iOS Application Programming Guide** at: `http://developer.apple.com/library/ios/#documentation/iphone/conceptual/iphoneosprogrammingguide/Introduction/Introduction.html`.

Creating the iCloudExample application

Before we can proceed to create our `iCloudExample` application, we must first launch the Xcode development environment.

1. Launch Xcode from the `/Developer/Applications` folder.

2. Select the **Single View Application** template to use from the **Project** template dialog box.

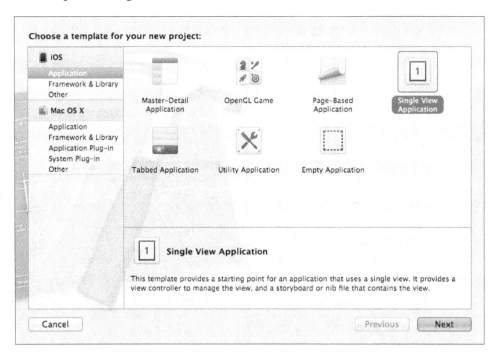

3. Then, click on the **Next** button to proceed to the next step in the Wizard. This will allow you to enter in the **Product Name** and your **Company Identifier**.

4. Enter in `iCloudExample` for the **Product Name**, and ensure that you have selected **iPhone** from the **Device Family** drop-down box.

5. Click on the **Next** button to proceed to the final step in the wizard.

6. Choose the folder location where you would like to save your project.

7. Click on the **Create** button to save your project at the location specified in *step 6*.

Once your project has been created, you will be presented with the Xcode development interface, along with the project files that the template created for you, within the **Project Navigator** window.

Our next step is to start building our user interface to obtain the Cloud URL, store keys, and documents within the Cloud, and look how to retrieve information from the Cloud:

1. Select the `iCloudExampleViewController.xib` file from within the `iCloudExample` folder within the **Project Navigator** window.

2. From the **Object Library**, select-and-drag a (`UIButton`) button control, onto the view.

3. Modify the **Object Attributes** of the button control, and set the title to read **Geti Cloud URL.**

4. Select-and-drag a (`UILabel`) label control, onto the view, and place it directly under the **Get iCloud URL** button.

5. Modify the **Object Attributes** of the label control, and set the **Text** property to read **iCloud URL:**.

Repeat the previous steps to add the buttons and labels for the **Store to iCloud**, **DocPath**, **Read from iCloud**, and **Item Value**.

If you have followed everything correctly, your view should look like the next screenshot. Feel free to adjust yours accordingly.

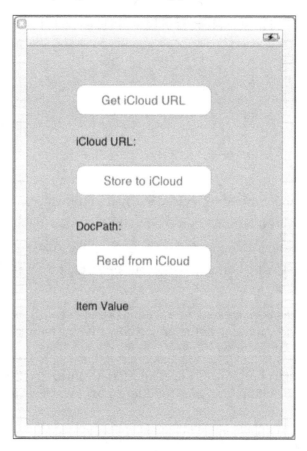

Now that we have created a user interface, you will need to bind up the controls to create the necessary events, and then follow these steps:

1. Open the `iCloudExampleViewController.h` interface file, located within the `iCloudExample` folder of your project, and add the following code:

```
#import<UIKit/UIKit.h>

@interfaceiCloudExampleViewController : UIViewController {
    UILabel *iCloudURL;
    UILabel *documentPath;
    UILabel *authorName;
}

- (IBAction)getCloudURL:(id)sender;
- (IBAction)storeDocument:(id)sender;
- (IBAction)readDocument:(id)sender;


@property (strong, nonatomic) IBOutletUILabel *iCloudURL;
@property (strong, nonatomic) IBOutletUILabel *documentPath;
@property (strong, nonatomic) IBOutletUILabel *authorName;

@end
```

2. Open our `iCloudExampleViewController.m` implementation file, located within the `iCloudExample` folder of your project, and add the following highlighted code:

```
#import "iCloudExampleViewController.h"
#import<Foundation/Foundation.h>
#import<Foundation/NSObject.h>

@implementationiCloudExampleViewController;

@synthesizeiCloudURL;
@synthesizedocumentPath;
@synthesizeauthorName;
```

 If we don't declare these, we will receive compiler-warning messages, which can result in unexpected results occurring in your application, or even make your application terminate unexpectedly.

3. Next, we need to declare the method that will connect to the iCloud service, using our TEAMID and the bundle identifier, and retrieve the iCloud URL. Enter in the following code snippet.

```
// Function to obtain the iCloud URL based on the TEAMID
// and the Bundle Identifier
- (IBAction)getCloudURL:(id)sender {
  // TeamID + Bundle Identifier
  NSFileManager *fileManager = [NSFileManagerdefaultManager];
  NSURL *CloudURL = [fileManager URLForUbiquityContainerIdentifier
    :@"TEAMID.com.yourcompany.iCloudExample"];

  iCloudURL.text = [@"iCloudURL = " stringByAppendingFormat:@"%@",
    [CloudURLabsoluteString ]];
  iCloudURL.numberOfLines = 4;
  iCloudURL.textColor = [UIColorblueColor];
}
```

When this button is executed, it will display the URL from your iCloud service, based on your TEAMID and bundle identifier.

```
file://localhost/private/var/mobile/Library/Mobile%20Documents/
TEAMID~com~yourcompany~iCloudExample/
```

4. Next, we need to implement our method that will be used to store a document into our iCloud sandbox. Enter in the following code snippet :

```
- (IBAction)storeDocument:(id)sender {
  // Store document in the Cloud
  NSArray *searchPath = NSSearchPathForDirectoriesInDomains(
    NSDocumentDirectory, NSUserDomainMask, YES);

  NSString *docPath = [searchPath objectAtIndex:0];
  NSString *fileName = [NSStringstringWithFormat:
    @"%@/iCloudExample.doc",docPath];
  NSString *fileContent = @"Welcome to storing documents using
    icloud. iCloud Rocks!!!";

  // Now Save the content to the documents directory
  [fileContentwriteToFile:fileNameatomically:
    NOencoding:NSStringEncodingConversionAllowLossyerror:nil];
  NSURL *fileURL = [NSURL URLWithString:fileName];

  documentPath.text = [@"DocPath = " stringByAppendingFormat:
    @"%@", [fileURLabsoluteString ]];
  documentPath.textColor = [UIColorblueColor];
  documentPath.lineBreakMode = UILineBreakModeWordWrap;
}
```

When this button is executed, this will display the path to the documents folder, located within the iCloud application sandbox:`/var/mobile/Applications/6BF2CE1F-C184-43FA-8D00-E4D476F8A538/Documents/iCloudExample.doc`.

5. Next, if you open the **Organizer** window, by selecting **Window | Organizer**, you will notice that our `iCloudExample.doc` has been added to our application sandbox.

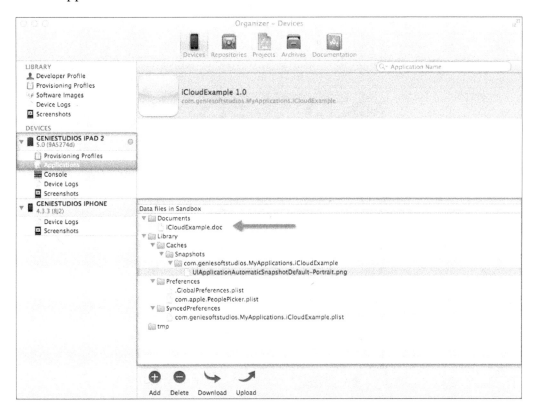

6. Next, we need to implement our method that will be used to add and retrieve key-value with our iCloud repository.

```
- (IBAction)readAuthor:(id)sender {

    NSUbiquitousKeyValueStore *cloudStore =
        [NSUbiquitousKeyValueStoredefaultStore];
    [cloudStoresetString:@"John Grisham" forKey:@"FavoriteAuthor"];

    // Important, as it first stores your in memory key values
    // to disk based storage, prior to eventually storing this
    //within iCloud
    [cloudStore synchronize];
```

```
    // Get the latest values from iCloud
    authorName.text = [@"Favorite Author = " stringByAppendingFormat
      :@"%@", [cloudStorestringForKey:@"FavoriteAuthor"]];
    authorName.textColor = [UIColorredColor];
    authorName.lineBreakMode = UILineBreakModeWordWrap;
}
```

When this button is executed, this will display the key entry value for our **Favorite Author** key-value data, located within the iCloud application sandbox: **Favorite Author = John Grisham**.

7. We are now ready to build and compile our `iCloudExample` application. The following screenshot shows the output when each of the buttons is pressed:

So there you have it, we have successfully created a simple, yet powerful application that can communicate with iCloud to store documents and key-value data, and retrieve the data from the Cloud.

Moving a document to iCloud storage

When moving documents to iCloud, you have the ability to create additional subdirectories from within the container directory to manage your files.

From a development point of view, it is recommended that when adding your documents to iCloud, you should create a Documents subdirectory and use that directory for storing user documents. Within iCloud, the contents of the Documents directory are made visible to the user so that individual documents can be deleted, whereas, everything outside of the Documents directory is grouped together, and treated as a single entity that a user can keep or delete.

The following code snippet creates and saves the file locally within your application sandbox first, before moving the file to the specified destination within iCloud.

```
// TeamID + Bundle Identifier
NSFileManager *fileManager = [NSFileManagerdefaultManager];
NSURL *CloudURL = [fileManager URLForUbiquityContainerIdentifier:
@"TEAMID.com.yourcompany.iCloudExample"];

NSString *docString = @"Documents";
NSURL *tempURL = [NSURL URLWithString:docString];
BOOL myVal = [fileManagersetUbiquitous:YESitemAtURL:
fileURLdestinationURL:CloudURLerror:NULL];
```

In this code snippet, we create an NSURL object that specifies the destination of the file within the user's iCloud storage. We then make a call to the URLForUbiquityContainerIdentifier: method of the NSFileManager classto get the root URL for the directory, and then append any additional directory and filenames to that URL. Finally, we call the setUbiquitous:itemAtURL:destinationURL:error: method of NSFileManager, to move the file to the specified destination in iCloud.

iCloud storage APIs

The iCloud storage APIs let your application write user documents and data to a central location, and access those items from all of a user's computers and iOS devices.

 Making a user's documents ubiquitous using iCloud, means that a user can view or edit those documents from any device without having to sync or transfer files explicitly.

Storing documents in a user's iCloud account provides a layer of security for that user. If the user happens to lose their device, any documents that were saved on it can easily be recovered if they are contained within iCloud storage. There are two ways to utilize iCloud storage, each with its own significant purpose. These are explained in the following table:

Storage type	Description
iCloud document storage	Use this feature to store user documents and data in the user's iCloud account. Refer to the section *Storing and using documents in iCloud*, located within this chapter.
iCloud key-value data storage	Use this feature to share small amounts of data among instances of your application. Refer to the section *Storing Key-Value data in iCloud*, located within this chapter.

Most applications that you create will use the iCloud document storage to share documents from a user's iCloud account. This will provide the ability to share documents across multiple devices, and manage documents from a given device.

When using the iCloud key-value data store, this is not something that a user will see, as this is handled your application and shares only small amounts of information; this information is used only by the application. An example of this would be that you can store the time the user logged in to your application, or what screen they are currently viewing.

The following screenshot shows the process involved when creating information within local iCloud storage, within your application's sandbox.

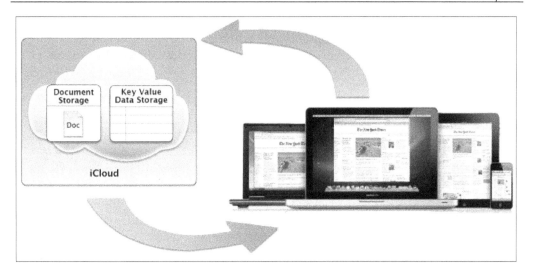

 For more information on how to go about storing and using documents within iCloud, refer to the section *Storing and using documents in iCloud*, located within this chapter.

Searching for documents in iCloud

There may be times when you need to check to see if a document exists at a location within the Cloud, prior to modifying the document. An example would be, say you wanted to check if a document existed prior to opening it within your application. If you don't perform a check and try to open this, you will receive an error.

Another case could be that you need to remove a file from your iCloud repository; you would still need to perform a check to ensure that the document indeed exists prior to attempting to remove this file, otherwise you will receive an improperly handled error, resulting in your application crashing.

To achieve any of these case scenarios, you will need to search the iCloud repository using the NSMetadataQuery object. Searching through the iCloud repository is a guaranteed way to locate documents, both in a user's iCloud storage and from within your application sandbox.

You should always use query objects instead of saving URLs persistently, because the user can delete files from iCloud storage when your application is not running. Using a query to search is the only way to ensure an accurate list of documents.

```
NSMetadataQuery *mdQuery = [[NSMetadataQueryalloc] init];
[mdQuerysetPredicate:[NSPredicatepredicateWithFormat:@"(kMDItemFSName
LIKE 'iCloudDoc *')"]];
[[NSNotificationCenterdefaultCenter] addObserver:selfselector:
@selector(processQuery:) name:nilobject:mdQuery];


[mdQuerystartQuery];
```

The following code snippet displays the associated `processQuery` method of the `NSNotification` class, and shows how we can perform and handle comparisons for each of the various `NSMetadataQuery` notification methods.

```
- (void)processQuery:(NSNotification *)notification {
NSMetadataQuery *mdQuery = [notification object];
if ([[notification name] isEqualToString:
NSMetadataQueryDidStartGatheringNotification]) {
NSLog(@"%@ %@ Query started", [self class],
NSStringFromSelector(_cmd));
}
else if ([[notification name] isEqualToString:
NSMetadataQueryGatheringProgressNotification]) {
NSLog(@"%@ %@ %ld", [self class],
NSStringFromSelector(_cmd), (long)[mdQueryresultCount]);
}
else if ([[notification name] isEqualToString:
NSMetadataQueryDidFinishGatheringNotification]) {
NSUIntegertheResultCount = [mdQueryresultCount];
theResultCount = 20;
for (NSUIntegeri; i<theResultCount; i++) {
NSLog(@"%@ %@ %ld %@", [self class],
NSStringFromSelector(_cmd), (long)i,
[mdQueryresultAtIndex:i]);
}
}
else {
NSLog(@"%@ %@ NSMetadataQueryDidUpdateNotification: %@",
[self class], NSStringFromSelector(_cmd), notification);
}
}
```

In iOS 5.0, the `NSMetadataQuery` class supports several search scopes for your documents. This is shown in the following table.

NSMetadataQueryclass methods	Description
`NSMetadataQueryUbiquitousDocumentsScope`	Use this feature to search for documents in iCloud that reside inside a documents directory (for any given container directory, put documents that the user is allowed to access inside a documents subdirectory).
`NSMetadataQueryUbiquitousDataScope`	Use this feature to search for documents in iCloud that reside anywhere other than in a documents directory (for any given container directory, use this scope to store user-related data files that your application needs to share, but are not files you want the user to manipulate directly).

Working with documents in iCloud

When your application needs to read or write a document in iCloud, it must do so in a coordinated manner. Your application might not be the only application trying to manipulate the local file at any given moment. The daemon that transfers the document to and from iCloud also needs to monitor the file periodically. To prevent your application from interfering with the daemon (and vice versa), iOS provides a coordinated locking mechanism that works with the files and directories you target for iCloud storage.

At the heart of the iCloud locking mechanism are file coordinators and file presenters.

The file coordinator

Whenever you need to read and write a file, you do so using a file coordinator, which is an instance of the `NSFileCoordinator` class. The job of a file coordinator is to coordinate the reads and writes performed by your application and the sync daemon on the same document. For example, your application and the daemon may both read the document at the same time, but only one may write to the file at any single time.

Also, if one process is reading the document, the other process is prevented from writing to the document, until the earlier process is finished reading the document.

The file presenter

In addition to coordinating operations, file coordinators also work with file presenters to notify applications when changes are about to occur. A file presenter is any object that conforms to the NSFilePresenter protocol, and takes responsibility for managing a specific file (or directory of files) in an application.

The job of a file presenter is to protect the integrity of its own data structures. It does this by listening for messages from other file coordinators and using those messages to update its internal data structures. In most cases, a file presenter may not have to do anything. However, if a file coordinator declares that it is about to move a file to a new URL, the file presenter would need to replace its old URL with the new one provided to it by the file coordinator.

Handling file-version conflicts

Handling version conflicts of files is a common issue in software development. With iCloud, we need to be able to handle this when multiple instances of your application are running on multiple devices, and both try to modify the same document. This will result in a conflict when both devices try to upload the changes made to the file at the same time.

At this point, iCloud will end up with two different versions of the same file, and has to decide what to do with them. Its solution is to make the most recently modified file the current file, and to mark any other versions of the file as conflict versions.

To avoid loss of changes made to those documents, your application will need to prompt the user to choose the appropriate course of action to take. For example, you might let the user choose which version of the file to keep, or you might offer to save the older version under a new name.

You would need to determine the current files, version, using the currentVersionOfItemAtURL: class method, and then obtain an array of the conflicted versions, by using the class method call to unresolvedConflictVersionsOfItemAtURL:.

For each conflicted file version, you will need to perform the appropriate cause of action to resolve the conflict, by using any of these actions, listed as follows:

- Merge the conflicted versions with the current file automatically, if this is practical to do so.

- Choose to ignore the conflicted versions, which will result in data being lost in those files.

- Prompt the user to select the appropriate course of action, and decide which of the versions that they should indeed keep. This should always be your last course of action.

Using iCloud storage responsibly

Applications that take advantage of iCloud storage features should act responsibly when storing data. The space available in each user's account is limited and is shared by all applications. In addition, users can see how much space is consumed by a given application, and choose to delete documents and data associated with that particular application. For these reasons, it is in your application's interest to be responsible about what files you store. Here are some tips to help you manage documents appropriately:

- Rather than storing all documents, let a user choose which documents to store in an iCloud account. If a user creates a large number of documents, storing all of those documents in iCloud could overwhelm that user's available space. Providing a way for a user to designate which documents to store in iCloud, gives that user more flexibility in deciding how best to use the available space.

- Remember that deleting a document removes it from a user's iCloud account and from all of that user's computers and devices. Make sure that users are aware of this fact and confirm any delete operations. For your application to remove the local copy of a document, and then download a fresh copy from iCloud, use the `evictUbiquitousItemAtURL:error:` method of `NSFileManager`.

- When storing documents in iCloud, place them in a documents directory whenever possible. Documents inside a documents directory can be deleted individually by the user to free up space. However, everything outside that directory is treated as data, and must be deleted all at once.

- Never store caches or other files that are private to your application in a user's iCloud storage. A user's iCloud account should only be used for storing user data and content.

- Treat files in iCloud the same way you treat all other files in your application sandbox. The time at which to save a file should be driven by the need of your application, and the need to preserve the user's data. You should not change your application to save files more or less frequently for iCloud. iCloud automatically optimizes its transfers to the server to ensure the best possible performance.

iCloud secures your content by encrypting it using SSL, when it is being sent over the internet. This results in your content being stored in encrypted format, and uses secure tokens for authentication.

 For more information on how to go about storing and using documents within iCloud, refer to the section *Storing and using documents in iCloud*, located within this chapter.

Summary

In this chapter, we learned about the benefits of using iCloud, and how to access them through their storage APIs. We looked at how we can incorporate iCloud features within our code, how to store and retrieve key-value data, and how to store documents within a folder inside our application sandbox.

We also learned about the process involved in how to search and locate a document within an iCloud repository, as well as learned to handle and avoid file-version conflicts when multiple copies of the same file are being updated on more than one device, and then being submitted to the iCloud repository.

In the next chapter, we will learn about the new debugging features of OpenGL ES, and how this new debugger in Xcode allows you to track-down issues specific to OpenGL ES directly within your code, right from within the IDE.

3
Debugging with OpenGL ES

The **Open Graphics Library (OpenGL)** can be simply defined as a *software interface to the graphics hardware*. It is a 3D graphics and modeling library that is highly portable and extremely fast. Using the OpenGL graphics API, you can create some brilliant graphics that are capable of representing 2D and 3D data.

The OpenGL library is a multi-purpose, open-source graphics library that supports applications for 2D and 3D digital content creation, mechanical and architectural design, virtual prototyping, flight simulation, and video games, and allows application developers to configure a 3D graphics pipeline, and submit data to it.

An object is defined by connected vertices. The vertices of the object are then transformed, lit, and assembled into primitives, and rasterized to create a 2D image that can be directly sent to the underlying graphics hardware to render the drawing, which is deemed to be typically very fast, due to the hardware being dedicated to processing graphics commands.

OpenGL for Embedded Systems (OpenGL ES) is a simplified version of the popular OpenGL framework that has been developed to be much easier to learn and implement, eliminating the need for redundant functionality within the iOS graphics hardware. This framework has been optimized to take full advantage of hardware-accelerated mathematical operations, so that developers can get the best performance.

In this chapter, we will be focusing on the new debugging features that come with the OpenGL ES debugger that enables developers to track down issues specific to OpenGL ES in your code.

In this chapter we will:

- Learn about the new workflow feature within Xcode 4
- Create a simple project to debug an OpenGL ES application
- Familiarize ourselves with the OpenGL ES 2.0 programmable pipeline
- Compile and link shaders into an OpenGL ES program
- Pass data from an application to shaders, using uniforms and attributes
- Detect OpenGL ES State information (view textures and shaders)
- Set and use breakpoints to catch OpenGL ES errors
- Set conditional OpenGL ES entry point breakpoints
- Break on frame boundaries

We have some fantastic stuff to cover in this chapter, so let's get started.

Understanding the new workflow feature within Xcode

In this section, we will be taking a look at the improvements that have been made to the Xcode 4 development environment, and how this can enable us to debug OpenGL ES applications much easier, compared to the previous versions of Xcode.

We will look at how we can use the frame capture feature of the debugger to capture all frame objects that are included within an OpenGL ES application. This tool enables you to list all the frame objects that are currently used by your application at a given point of time.

We will familiarize ourselves with the new OpenGL ES debugger within Xcode, to enable us to track down specific issues relating to OpenGL ES within the code.

Creating a simple project to debug an OpenGL ES application

Before we can proceed, we first need to create our OpenGLESExample project. To refresh your memory, you can refer to the section that we covered in *Chapter 2*, under the section *Creating the iCloudExample application*:

1. Launch Xcode from the /Developer/Applications folder.
2. Select the **OpenGL Game** template from the **Project** template dialog box.

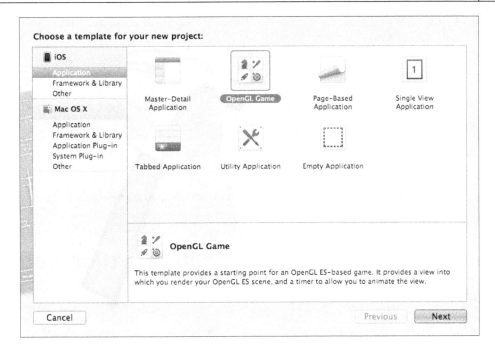

3. Then, click on the **Next** button to proceed to the next step in the wizard. This will allow you to enter in the **Product Name** and your **Company Identifier**.

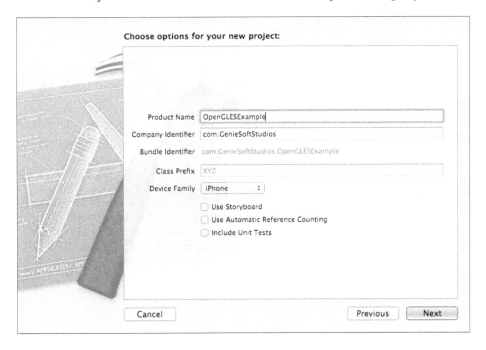

4. Enter in `OpenGLESExample` for the **Product Name**, and ensure that you have selected **iPhone** from the **Device Family** dropdown box.

5. Next, click on the **Next** button to proceed to the final step in the wizard.

6 Choose the folder location where you would like to save your project.

7. Then, click on the **Create** button to save your project at the location specified.

Once your project has been created, you will be presented with the Xcode development interface, along with the project files that the template created for you within the Project **Navigator** window.

Now that we have our project created, we need to configure our project to enable us to debug the state of the objects.

Detecting OpenGL ES state information and objects

To enable us to detect and monitor the state of the objects within our application, we need to enable this feature through the **Edit Scheme...** section of our project, as shown in the following screenshot:

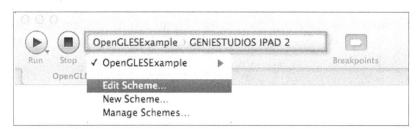

From the **Edit Scheme** section, as shown in the following screenshot, select the **Run OpenGLESExampleDebug** action, then click on the **Options** tab, and then select the **OpenGL ES Enable** frame capture checkbox.

For this feature to work, you must run the application on an iOS device, and the device must be running iOS 5.0 or later. This feature will not work within the iOS simulator. You will need to ensure that after you have attached your device, you will then need to restart Xcode for this option to become available.

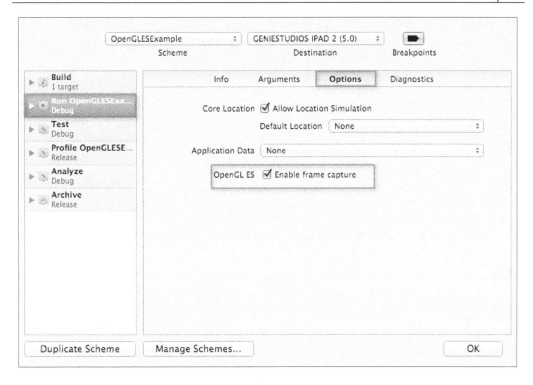

When you have configured your project correctly, click on the **OK** button to accept the changes made, and close the dialog box. Next, build and run your OpenGL ES application. When you run your application, you will see two three-dimensional and colored box cubes.

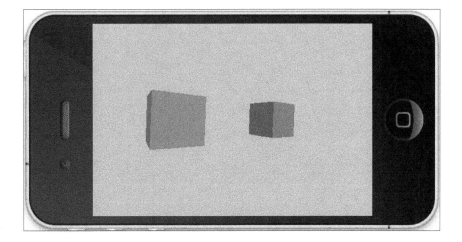

When you run your application on the iOS device, you will notice that the frame capture appears within the Xcode 4 debug bar, as shown in the following screenshot:

When using the OpenGL ES features of Xcode 4.2, these debugging features enable you to do the following:

1. Inspect OpenGL ES state information.
2. Introspect OpenGL ES objects such as view textures and shaders.
3. Step through draw calls and watch changes with each call.
4. Step through the state calls that proceed each draw call to see exactly how the image is constructed.

The following screenshot displays the captured frame of our sample application. The debug navigator contains a list of every draw call and state call associated with that particular frame.

The buffers that are associated with the frame are shown within the editor pane, and the state information is shown in the debug windowpane. The default view when the OpenGL ES frame capture is launched is displayed in the **Auto** view. This view displays the color portion, which is the Renderbuffer #1, as well as its grayscale equivalent of the image, that being Renderbuffer #2.

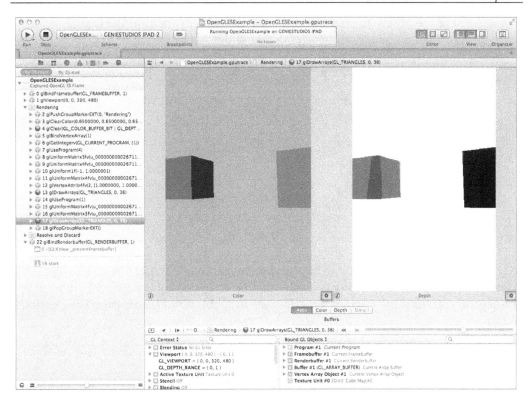

You can also toggle the visibility between each of the channels for red, green and blue, as well as the alpha channels, and then use the **Range** scroll to adjust the color range. This can be done easily by selecting each of the cog buttons, shown in the previous screenshot.

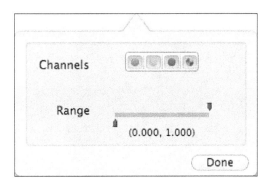

You also have the ability to step through each of the draw calls in the debug navigator, or by using the double arrows and slider in the debug bar.

When using the draw call arrows or sliders, you can have Xcode select the stepped-to draw call from the debug navigator. This can be achieved by *Control* + clicking below the captured frame, and choosing the **Reveal in Debug Navigator** from the shortcut menu.

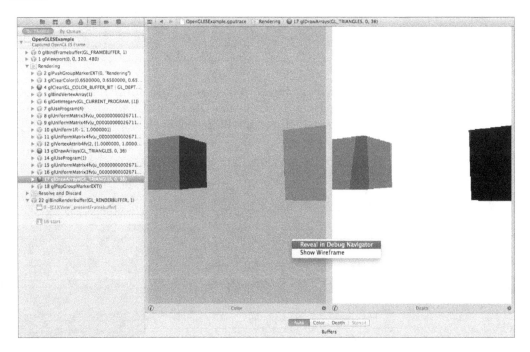

You can also use the shortcut menu to toggle between the standard view of drawing the image, as well as showing the wireframe view of the object, by selecting the **Show Wireframe** option from the pop-up menu, as shown in the previous screenshot.

When using the wireframe view of an object, it highlights the element that is being drawn by the selected draw call. To turn off the wireframe feature and have the image return back to the normal state, select the **Hide Wireframe** option from the pop-up menu, as shown in the following screenshot:

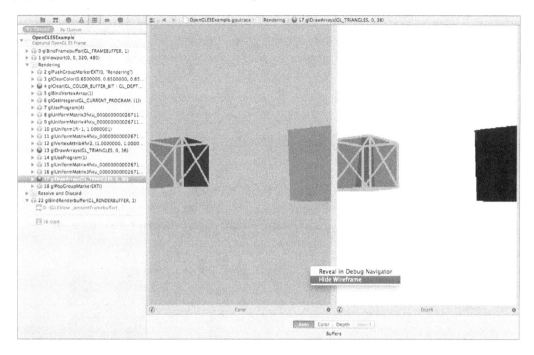

Now that you have a reasonable understanding of debugging through an OpenGL ES application and its draw calls, let's take a look at how we can view the textures associated with an OpenGL ES application.

View textures

When referring to textures in OpenGL ES 2.0, this is basically an image that can be sampled by the graphics engine pipeline, and is used to map a colored image onto a mapping surface. To view objects that have been captured by the frame capture button, follow these simple steps:

1. Open the **Assistant Editor** to see the objects associated with the captured frame. In this view, you can choose to see all of the objects, only bound objects, or the stack. This can be accessed from the **View | Assistant Editor | Show Assistant Editor** menu, as shown in the following screenshot:

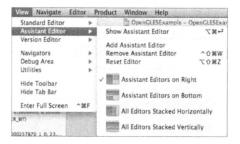

2. Open a secondary assistant editor pane, so that you can see both the objects and the stack frame at the same time. This can be accessed from the **View | Assistant Editor | Add Assistant Editor** menu shown previously, or by clicking on the **+** symbol, as shown in the following screenshot:

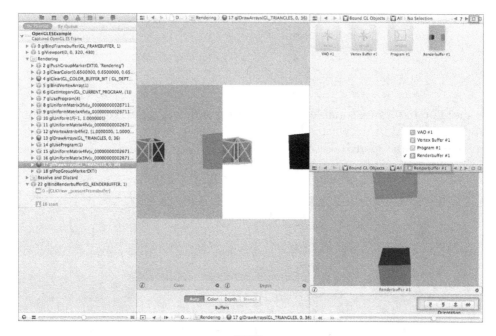

To see details about any object contained within the OpenGL ES assistant editor, double-click on the object, or choose the item from the pop-up list, as shown in the following screenshot:

It is worth mentioning that, from within this view, you have the ability to change the orientation of any object that has been captured and has been rendered to the view. To change the orientation, locate the **Orientation** options shown at the bottom-right hand of the screen. Objects can be changed to appear in one or more views as needed, and these are as follows:

- Rotate clockwise
- Rotate counter-clockwise
- Flip orientation vertically
- Flip orientation horizontally

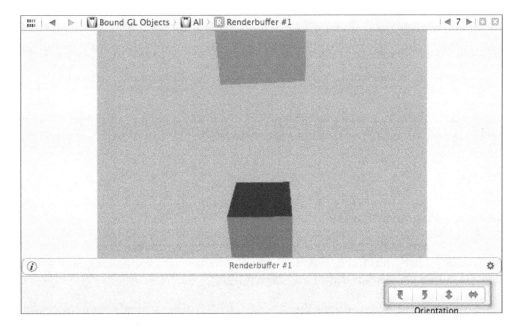

For example, if you want to see information about the **vertex array object (VAO)**, you would double-click on it to see it in more detail, as shown in the following screenshot.

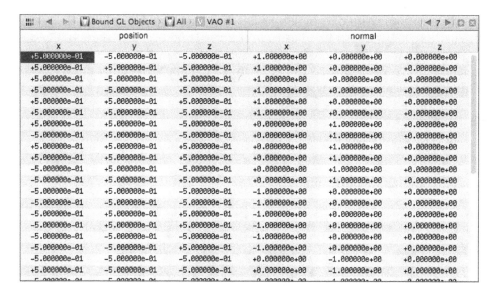

This displays all the x, y, and z-axes required to construct each of our objects. Next, we will take a look into how shaders are constructed.

Shaders

There are two types of shaders that you can write for OpenGL ES; these are **Vertex shaders** and **Fragment shaders**.

These two shaders make up what is known as the **Programmable** portion of the OpenGL ES 2.0 programmable pipeline, and are written in a C-like language syntax, called **The OpenGL ES Shading Language** (GLSL).

The following screenshot outlines the OpenGL ES 2.0 programmable pipeline, and combines a version of the OpenGL Shading Language for programming **Vertex Shader** and **Fragment Shader** that has been adapted for embedded platforms for iOS devices:

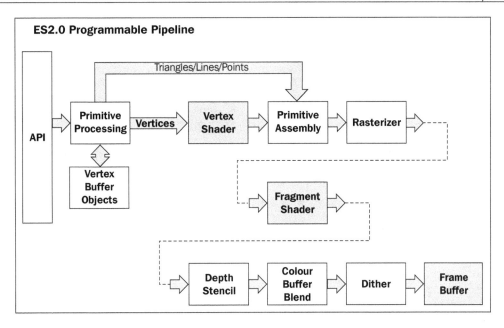

Shaders are not new, these have been used in a variety of games that use OpenGL. Such games that come to mind are: Doom 3 and Quake 4, or several flight simulators, such as Microsoft's Flight Simulator X.

Once thing to note about shaders, is that they are not compiled when your application is built. The source code of the shader gets stored within your application bundle as a text file, or defined within your code as a string literal, that is,
```
vertShaderPathname = [[NSBundlemainBundle]
pathForResource:@"Shader" ofType:@"vsh"];
```

Before you can use your shaders, your application has to load and compile each of them. This is done to preserve device independence.

Let's take for example, if Apple decided to change to a different GPU manufacturer, for future releases of its iPhone, the compiled shaders may not work on the new GPU. Having your application deferring the compilation to runtime will avoid this problem, and any latest versions of the GPU will be fully supported without a need for you to rebuild your application.

The following table explains the differences between the two shaders.

Shader type	Description
Vertex shaders	These are programs that get called once-per-vertex in your scene. An example to explain this better would be - if you were rendering a simple scene with a single square, with one vertex at each corner, this would be called four times.
	Their job is to perform some calculations such as lighting, geometry transforms, moving, scaling and rotating of objects, to simulate realism.
Fragment shaders	These are programs that get called once-per-pixel in your scene. So, if you're rendering that same simple scene with a single square, it will be called once for each pixel that the square covers. Fragment shaders can also perform lighting calculations, and so on, but their most important job is to set the final color for the pixel.

Next, we will start by examining the implementation of the vertex shader that the OpenGL template created for us. You will notice that these shaders are code files that have been implemented using C-Syntax like instructions. Lets, start by examining each section of the vertex shader file, by following these simple steps:

1. Open the Shader.vsh vertex shader file located within the OpenGLESExample folder of the **Project Navigator** window, and examine the following code snippet.

```
attribute vec4 position;
attribute vec3 normal;

varying lowp vec4 colorVarying;
uniform mat4 modelViewProjectionMatrix;
uniform mat3 normalMatrix;

void main(){
  vec3 eyeNormal = normalize(normalMatrix * normal);
  vec3 lightPosition = vec3(0.0, 0.0, 1.0);
  vec4 diffuseColor = vec4(0.4, 0.4, 1.0, 1.0);

  floatnDotVP = max(0.0, dot(eyeNormal,
    normalize(lightPosition)));

  colorVarying = diffuseColor * nDotVP;
  gl_Position = modelViewProjectionMatrix * position;
}
```

2. Next, we will take a look at what this piece of code is doing and explain what is actually going on. So let's start.

   The attribute keyword declares that this shader is going to be passed in an input variable called `position`. This will be used to indicate the position of the vertex. You will notice that the `position` variable has been declared of type `vec4`, which means that each vertex contains four floating-point values. The second attribute input variable that is declared with the variable name `normal`, has been declared of type `vec3`, which means that the vertex contains three floating-point values that are used for the rotational aspect around the x, y, and z axes.

   The third attribute input variable that is declared with the variable name `diffuseColor`, defines the color to be used for the vertex. We declare another variable called `colorVarying`. You will notice that it doesn't contain the `attribute` keyword. This is because it is an output variable that will be passed to the fragment shader.

   The varying keyword tells us the value for a particular vertex. This basically means that you can specify a different color for each vertex, and it will make all the values in-between a neat gradient that you will see in the final output. We have declared this as `vec4`, because colors are comprised of four component values.

3. Finally, we declare two uniform keyword variables called `modelViewProjectionMatrix` and `normalMatrix`. The model, view, and projection matrices are three separate matrices. Model maps from an object's local coordinate space into world space, view from world space to camera space, and projection from camera to screen.

   When all three are used, you can then use the one result to map all the way from object space to screen space, enabling you to work out what you need to pass on to the next stage of a programmable pipeline from the incoming vertex positions.

   The normal matrix vectors are used to determine how much light is received at the specified vertex or surface. Uniforms are a second form of data that allow you to pass from your application code to the shaders. Uniform types are available to both vertex and fragment shaders, which, unlike attributes, are only available to the vertex shader.

 The value of a uniform cannot be changed by the shaders, and will have the same value every time a shader runs for a given trip through the pipeline. Uniforms can also contain any kind of data that you want to pass along for use in your shader.

4. Next, we assign the value from the color per-vertex attribute to the varying variable `colorVarying`. This value will then be available in the fragment shader in interpolated form.

5. Finally, we modify the `gl_Position` output variable, using the floating point translate variable to move the vertex along the X, Y, and Z-axes, based on the value of the translate uniform.

   Next, we will take a look at the fragment shader that the OpenGL ES template created for us.

6. Open the `Shader.fsh` fragment shader file located within the **OpenGLESExample** folder of the **Project Navigator** window, and examine the following code snippet.

```
varying lowp vec4 colorVarying;

void main(){
  gl_FragColor = colorVarying;
}
```

We will now take a look at this code snippet, and explain what is actually going on here.

You will notice that within the fragment shader, the declaration of the varying type variable `colorVarying`, as highlighted in the code, has the same name as it did in the vertex shader. This is very important; if these names were different, OpenGL ES won't realize it's the same variable, and your program will produce unexpected results.

The type is also very important, and it has to be the same data type as it was declared within the vertex shader. This is a GLSL keyword that is used to specify the precision of the number of bytes used to represent a number.

From a programming point of view, the more bytes that are used to represent a number, the fewer problems you will be likely to have with the rounding of floating point calculations. GLSL allows the user to precision modifiers any time a variable is declared, and it must be declared within this file. Failure to declare it within the fragment shader, will result in your shader failing to compile.

The `lowp` keyword is going to give you the best performance with the least accuracy during interpolation. This is the better option when dealing with colors, where small rounding errors don't matter. Should you find the need to increase the precision, it is better to use the `mediump` or `highp`, if the lack of precision causes you problems within your application.

For more information on the **OpenGL ES Shading Language**
(GLSL) or the **Precision modifiers**, refer to the following
documentation located at: `http://www.khronos.org/registry/`
`gles/specs/2.0/GLSL_ES_Specification_1.0.17.pdf`.

Error handling in OpenGL ES

OpenGL provides simple error-handling routines for the base GL and GLU libraries.
You can use the function `glGetError` to check for errors. OpenGL only records the
first error to occur. All subsequent errors are ignored, until the error buffer is cleared
by a call to `glGetError`.

The command that caused the error is ignored, so it has no effect on OpenGL state or
on the frame buffer contents. Once recorded, the current error code isn't cleared and
additional errors aren't recorded until you call the query command `glGetError()`,
which returns the current error code. After you've queried and cleared the current
error code, or if there's no error to begin with, `glGetError()` returns `GL_NO_ERROR`.
The syntax of the `glGetError` function is defined as follows:

```
GLenum glGetError (void);
```

The `glGetError` function returns the value of the error flag. When an error has been
detected in either the GL or GLU libraries, the error flag is set to the appropriate
error code value.

If `GL_NO_ERROR` is returned, there has been no detectable error since the
last call to `glGetError()`, or since the GL was initialized.

If no other errors are recorded until the `glGetError()` method is called,
the error code is returned, and the flag is reset to `GL_NO_ERROR`.

The following table lists the basic defined OpenGL error codes and their descriptions
that are returned by the `glGetError` method call.

Error code	Description
`GL_INVALID_ENUM`	GLenum argument out of range
`GL_INVALID_VALUE`	Numeric argument out of range
`GL_INVALID_OPERATION`	Operation illegal in current state
`GL_STACK_OVERFLOW`	Command would cause a stack overflow
`GL_STACK_UNDERFLOW`	Command would cause a stack underflow
`GL_OUT_OF_MEMORY`	Not enough memory left to execute command
`GL_NO_ERROR`	No error has occurred.

Detecting errors by setting up breakpoints

Setting breakpoints within your code gives you the flexibility to stop execution at any point within your code, so that you can investigate and step through to find out why a piece of code is not working correctly. This is particularly handy if you want to step through specific OpenGL functions. These breakpoints should be set immediately before calling the function, and your program will be stopped and the status bar will indicate which function caused the breakpoint.

Setting up breakpoints in your code

Although you can use the debugger to pause execution of your program at any time and view the state of the running code, it's usually helpful to set breakpoints before running your executable so that you can stop at known points, and view the values of variables in your source code.

A breakpoint is basically an instruction in your code that tells the application to *stop* when the breakpoint is reached, and execution of the program pauses, waiting for further instructions as to what to do next. During this phase, you have the opportunity to either inspect the current values of any of the properties, or step through the code.

Let's take a look at the following routine that uses the glGetError method.

```
- (void)startAnimation{
  if (!animating) {
    CADisplayLink *aDisplayLink = [[UIScreenmainScreen]
      displayLinkWithTarget:self selector:@selector(drawFrame)];
    [aDisplayLinksetFrameInterval:animationFrameInterval];
    [aDisplayLinkaddToRunLoop:[NSRunLoopcurrentRunLoop]
      forMode:NSDefaultRunLoopMode];
    self.displayLink = aDisplayLink;
      GLenum err;
      err = glGetError();
      while ( GL_NO_ERROR != err ) {
        NSLog(@"Error. glError: 0x%04X", err);
        err = glGetError();
      }
    animating = YES;
  }
}
```

You will notice that we have declared a variable `err`, which will be used to store the error number that will be returned by the `glGetError` method. We then cycle through and output each error message's details to the debug console window until no more errors exist, upon which, we exit from the loop. Although you can use the Xcode 4 debugger to pause execution of your program at any time to view the state of your running code, it is more helpful to set breakpoints at those areas prior to running your application.

To set breakpoints, open any source implementation file, and click within the gutter pane section of the Xcode source editor, next to the spot to where you would like your program to stop. When you add a breakpoint, Xcode will automatically enable it and this will be indicated by a light blue color as shown in the screenshot below. Breakpoints can also be toggled to be switched off, by clicking on the breakpoint again, having this turn to more of a transparent color.

The **Breakpoint Navigator** window shows all current breakpoints that have been set within your project, and will display all active as well as inactive breakpoints.

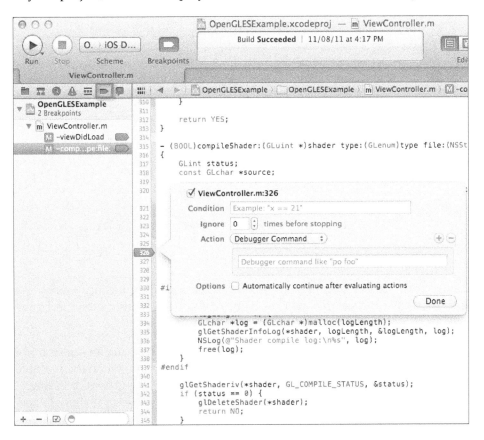

This view contains several options that can be configured for each breakpoint, and a breakpoint can contain multiple conditions. You can choose to log messages out to the Xcode console window, or execute a `debug` command. To access this view, hold down the *control* key, and right-click with the mouse.

A new feature that comes with Xcode 4.2, is the ability to capture OpenGL frames, so that you can debug your code right within the Xcode development environment, and scroll through each of your OpenGL ES method calls, as well as viewing state and objects.

Setting conditional OpenGL ES entry point breakpoints

We have looked at setting breakpoints within your code in the event that you want your application to stop whenever that particular line is hit. Another way in which you can use breakpoints, is to have them stop when a particular condition has been met, and then have it perform a particular action, as shown in following example:

You have the ability to either have it stop when the condition has been met, as seen in this screenshot, or you can choose to ignore the condition altogether and have it fire after a specified number of times the method gets called.

You can then choose to have it fire of a particular action. As you can see from this screenshot, we set up a condition to capture the current frame when the variable `transY` is greater than or equal to 2. This will then launch the **OpenGL Frame Capture** section, so that we can step through and debug our code further, to see what is going on.

There are other ways in which we can debug OpenGL ES projects through the use of **Instruments**, which we will be covering in *Chapter 6, Xcode Tools Improvements*.

Breaking on frame boundaries

The **OpenGL ES Debugger** allows you to see all of the frames that are being drawn within your application. You can have your application break at a certain point within your program, and then use the debug navigator to navigate to the area within your code to where the frame has been drawn. In the following screenshot, it displays the instance of the captured frame, and displays the state calls associated within that frame:

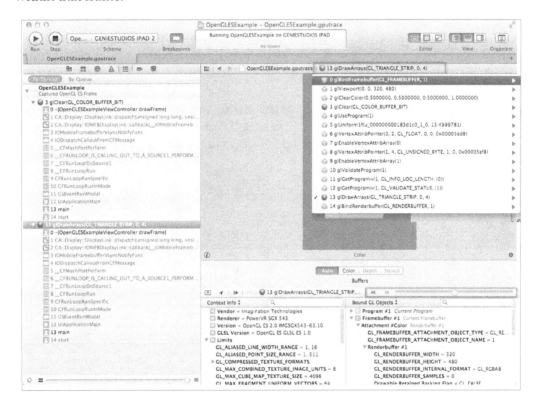

Selecting the `glDrawArrays(GL_TRIANGLE_STRIP, 0, 4)` option, as shown in the previous screenshot, will allow you to see a list of all of the associated draw calls that have been made. You can also cycle through the frames that have been captured by using the scrub bar, as highlighted in the previous screenshot.

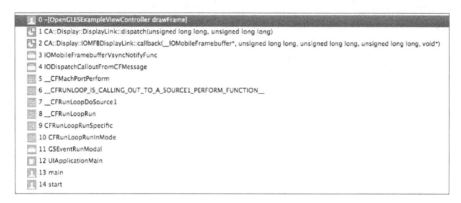

Clicking on the **[OpenGLESExampleViewController drawframe]** method , as shown in the previous screenshot, will open the Xcode development IDE and take you directly to the area to where your code is located, as shown in the following screenshot:

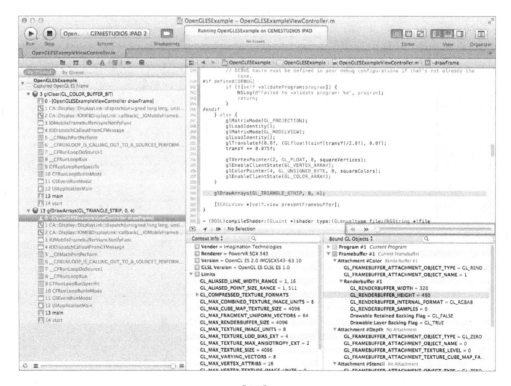

By using the OpenGL ES debugger, you can step through each of your frames within your application, to help you track-down and debug when textures are not rendering properly, or if the colors on your object look odd.

Summary

In this chapter, we learned about the differences between vertex shaders and fragment shaders, and their relation to one another. We then looked at the new debugging features of OpenGL ES, and how this new debugger in Xcode allows you to track down issues specific to OpenGL ES within your code, right within the Xcode IDE.

We familiarized ourselves with the OpenGL ES frame capture tool, its ability to stop execution of a program, and grab the current frame contents that are being rendered on the iOS device. This is so that we are able to easily track-down and correct program issues, by taking a closer look at the program state information of objects, by scrolling through the debug navigator stack trace, as well as the ability to see all of the textures and shaders currently being used by the application.

We also learned about the OpenGL ES `glGetError` method call, and how we can use this to provide us with a list of errors that have been detected. To end the chapter, we looked at how we can break on frame boundaries within OpenGL and see the values of the current program frame state, as defined by the objects.

In the next chapter, we will gain an understanding of what **Storyboards** are, and how we can apply the various transitions between views, as well as how to create and configure scenes and storyboard files, to present these programmatically. We will also look at how to build and integrate Twitter capabilities into our application, to tweet photos and standard messages.

4
Using Storyboards

Starting with the release of Xcode 4.2, developers and designers now have the ability to layout the workflow of their applications, using the new **Storyboards** feature that has been incorporated as part of Interface Builder. Storyboards can be used to build an in-game menu system for moving between different screens, or they can be used to build business applications that use the navigation and tab bars controls to transition between each of the different views, as they manage the view controllers created by the developer.

Previously, instead of creating numerous interface files, you can now start dragging and editing all your views in one place, with the ability to specify transitions between screens and the associated actions that trigger them. Storyboards also include a design pattern that can be implemented to send and receive data between controllers. In the previous instances, you would have had to implement protocols, delegates, notifications, or some other custom way to maintain state between screens.

In this chapter, we will be gaining an understanding into what Storyboards actually are, as well as familiarizing ourselves with the new workflow that has been implemented within Interface Builder. We will look at the steps involved to create storyboards and how to apply different transition techniques between each view, to create a Twitter application to post messages and photos.

In this chapter, we will:

- Gain an understanding into what Storyboards are
- Learn how to use Storyboards to create and configure transitions to scenes
- Create a simple storyboard application with Twitter integration
- Learn about the process involved to create storyboard files
- Post a tweet message and add a photo
- Programmatically transition to a new storyboard view-controller

We have some fantastic stuff to cover in this chapter, so let's get started.

Understanding Storyboards

In the past, when you needed to create a new view for your application, you would have had to create a new xib file for each of the views. This became very cumbersome when dealing with complex applications, as they contained a number of different views and became hard transitioning from one view controller to the next.

Apple decided to improve this in a big way, by substantially making improvements in this area regarding the user interface design process, by introducing a technique called **Storyboarding**.

Storyboarding is a feature that is built into Xcode 4.2, and later that allows both the various screens that comprise an iOS application and the navigation path through those screens to be visually assembled. When you use Storyboards, they enable you to design the application workflow of your screens, similarly to the way a movie director prepares storyboard sketches for every scene of a shoot.

You can then use Interface Builder to layout the parts for each of the screens graphically, as well as the transitions between them, and the controls used to trigger the transitions.

The following screenshot shows a simple storyboard application containing two view controllers with linkage between them.

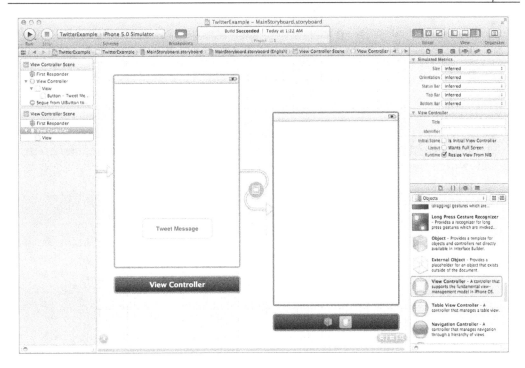

Transitions

Xcode provides the option to change the visual appearance of the transition that takes place from one scene to another within a storyboard, referred to as a **segue**. Using transitions enables you to apply a variety of different styles to each of your view controllers that are to be rendered and displayed to the view, and are represented by arrows between each of the view controllers. By default, a **Cover Vertical** transition is performed whereby the new scene slides vertically upwards from the bottom of the view to cover the currently displayed scene.

You may have seen such transitions in applications, such as the Photos app that comes part of the iPhone and iPad, where you can apply a transition and start a slideshow.

You also have the ability to define custom transitions that enable you to provide a custom segue class method to handle the transition. This can be achieved by selecting **Custom** for the style of the segue, and fill in the name of the custom segue class to use. To use any of the standard segue classes, these are located within the UIKit class.

For information relating to the standard segue classes, refer to the `UIKit` framework reference, located at the Apple developer connection website, using the following link: `http://developer.apple.com/library/ios/#documentation/uikit/reference/UIKit_Framework/_index.html`.

In order to configure a segue to specify a kind of transition to use between the different scenes, click on the segue and open the **Attributes** inspector, as shown in the following screenshot:

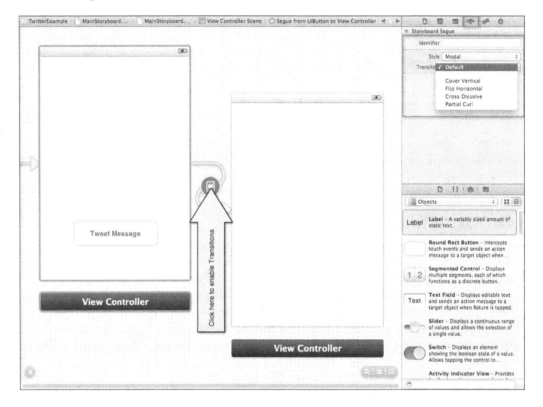

You have the ability to choose from the various transition types that are only applicable to the **Modal** style; these are explained within the following table:

Transition name	Description
Default	When this transition is selected, it uses the **Cover Vertical** transition style.
Cover Vertical	When the view controller is presented, its view slides up from the bottom of the screen. When the view is dismissed, it slides back down.
Flip Horizontal	When the view controller is presented, the current view initiates a horizontal 3D flip from right-to-left, resulting in the revealing of the new view as if it were on the back of the previous view. When this view is dismissed, the flip occurs from left-to-right, returning to the original view.
Cross Dissolve	When the view controller is presented, the current view fades-out while the new view fades-in at the same time. When the view is dismissed, a similar type of cross-fade is used to return to the original view.
Partial Curl	When the view controller is presented, one corner of the current view curls up to reveal the modal view underneath. When the view is dismissed, the curled up page uncurls itself back on top of the modal view. A modal view presented using this transition is itself prevented from presenting any additional modal views.
	This transition style is supported only if the parent view controller is presenting a full-screen view and you use the `UIModalPresentationFullScreen` modal presentation style. Attempting to use a different form factor for the parent view or a different presentation style triggers an exception.

For more information on the above transition types, refer to the `UIViewController` framework reference located on the Apple developer website, using the following link: `http://developer.apple.com/library/ios/#documentation/uikit/reference/UIViewController_Class/Reference/Reference.html`.

Now that we have an understanding of how to go about creating transitions for a view, our next step is to take a look at how we can create storyboards and how to configure scenes for our storyboard application.

How to go about creating Storyboard files

In the next section, we will take a look at how to go about creating a storyboard application. When you create a new storyboard file, this will give you a view controller object that represents your scene, which is the initial view controller.

Each view controller represents the contents of a single screen. When creating applications for the iPad, a screen can be composed of the contents of more than one scene and you link each object that is contained within a view controller, to another view controller that implements another scene.

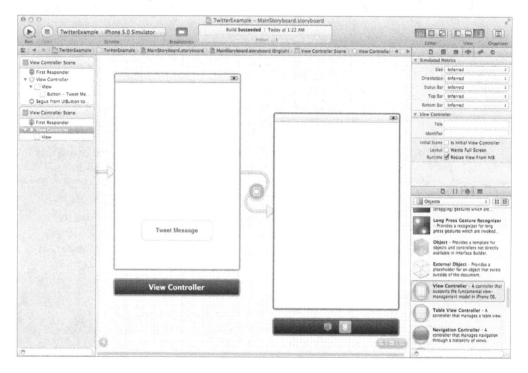

As you can see from this screenshot, the initial view controller contains a green outline. You link the various view controllers using Interface Builder by *Control* + dragging between controls and view controllers. You have the ability to add controls and views to each view controller's view, just as you would add objects to a window or a view in an XIB file.

Creating a simple Storyboard (Twitter) application

Before we can proceed, we first need to create our `TwitterExample` project. To refresh your memory, you can refer to the section that we covered in *Chapter 2, Creating the iCloudExample Application*.

1. Launch Xcode from the `/Developer/Applications` folder.

2. Choose **Create a new Xcode project**, or **File | New Project**.

3. Select the **Single View Application** template from the **Project template** dialog box.

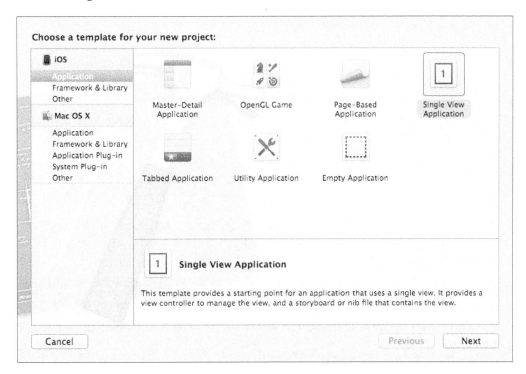

4. Then, click on the **Next** button to proceed to the next step in the Wizard. This will allow you to enter in the **Product Name** and your **Company Identifier**.

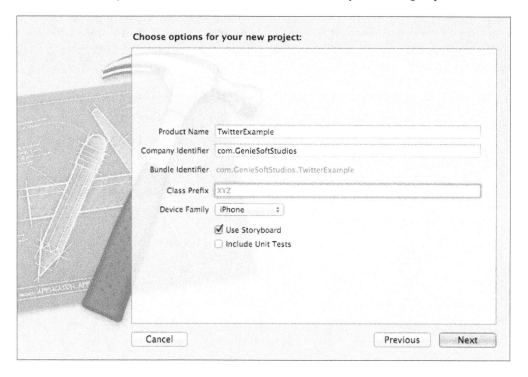

5. Enter in `TwitterExample` for the **Product Name**, and ensure that you have selected **iPhone** from the **Device Family** drop-down box, and that you have checked the **Use Storyboard** option.

6. Next, click on the **Next** button to proceed to the final step in the wizard.

7. Choose the folder location where you would like to save your project.

8. Then, click on the **Create** button to save your project at the location specified.

Once your project has been created, you will be presented with the Xcode development interface, along with the project files that the template created for you within the **Project Navigator** window. Our next step is to start building the user interface for our Twitter application.

Creating scenes

The process of creating scenes involves adding a new view controller to the storyboard, which is referred to as a **scene**. Each view controller is responsible for managing a single scene. A better way to describe scenes would be to think of the collection of scenes as a movie, where each frame that is being displayed is the actual scene that connects onto the next part.

When adding scenes to your storyboard file, you can add controls and views to the view controller's view, just as you would do for an XIB file, and have the ability to configure outlets and actions between your view controllers and its views.

To add a new scene into your storyboard file, follow these simple steps:

1. From the **Project Navigator**, select the file named `MainStoryboard.storyboard`.

2. From the **Object** library, select and drag a new view-controller on to the storyboard canvas. This is shown in the following screenshot:

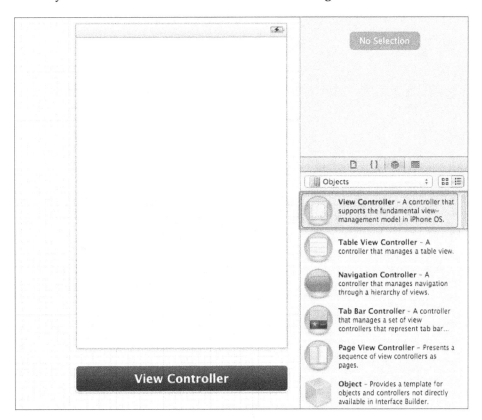

3. Next, drag a UIButton control on to the view that we will use in a later section to call the calling view. In the button's attributes, change the text to read Go Back.

4. Finally, on the first view controller, drag a UIButton control on to the view, just above the **Tweet Message** button. In the button's attributes, change the text to read About App. This will be used to call the new view that we added in the previous step.

   Once you have added the controls to each of the views, your final interface should look something like what is shown in the following screenshot.

5. Next, create the action event for the **About App** button; hold down the control key on your keyboard and drag the mouse from the **About App** button to the ViewController.h interface file.

6. Select **Action** from the **Connection** type drop-down, then enter in showAbout for the name of the IBAction method to create, and then click on the **Connect** button to accept the changes, as shown in the following screenshot:

Now that we have created our scene, buttons, and actions, our next step is to configure the scene, which is shown in the next section.

Configuring scenes

When you want to transition from one view controller to another, you can hold down the *Control* key and click a button, table view cell, or any other object from one view controller, and then drag it to the new view controller for a different scene. This technique of dragging between view controllers creates what is known as a **Segue**.

A segue is a configurable object that supports all of the same types of transitions made available to you within the UIKit class reference, such as modal transitions and navigation transitions.

You also have the ability to define custom transitions that replace one view controller with another. To create a segue and configure a scene, follow these simple steps:

1. Select the **About App** button with your mouse, and hold down the *Control* key while dragging it to the view controller for the scene that you would like to load when the button is selected.

2. Release the mouse button, and then choose the **Modal** option from the pop-up menu selection.

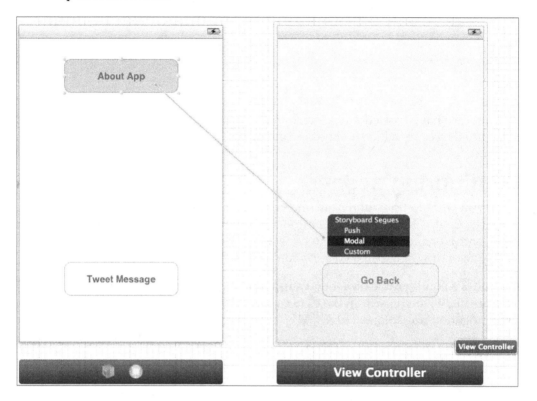

You will notice that a gray arrow connects both of your view controllers. When the **About App** button is pressed, it will display the page containing the **Go Back** button.

3. Next, we need to do the same for our second view, so that when the **Go Back** button is pressed, it will return back to our first view.

4. Repeat *steps 1* to *2*, but substitute the **Go Back** button for the **About App** button.

   Explanations of the Storyboard Segues that come part of Xcode 4 are included in the following table:

Segue name	Description
Modal	A modal view controller is not a specific subclass of the `UIViewController` class, as any type of view controller can be presented modally by your application. However, like the tab bar and navigation view controllers, you can present your view controllers modally when you want to convey a specific meaning about the relationship between the previous view hierarchy and the newly presented view hierarchy.
Push	**Push** segues allow you to push a new view controller onto the navigation stack, just as if you were stacking plates. The view at the top of the stack being the one that gets rendered.
Custom	These allow you to customize and call a view controller from code using the `prepareForSegue` method, and are what you use to present the content of your application.
	The job of the view controller is to manage the presentation of some content and coordinate the update and the synchronization of that content with the application's underlying data objects.
	In the case of a custom view controller, this involves creating a view to present the content and implementing the infrastructure needed to synchronize the contents of that view with your application's data structures.

Once you have done this, your view controllers should look like something shown in the next screenshot. You can apply a number of transitions to each of your view controllers, so that they can perform animation when they get displayed to the view.

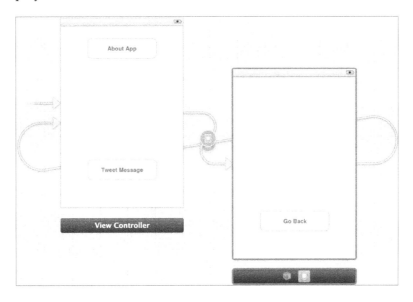

To learn how to apply transitions to your view controller, please refer to the section on *Transitions* in this chapter.

5. Now that you have applied each of the segues to both view controller, our final step is to compile, build, and run our application.

6. From the **Product** menu, select **Run**. Alternatively, press the **Command | R** keys to compile, build, and run the application.

The following screenshot shows our application running within the iOS simulator, with each of their associated screens displayed.

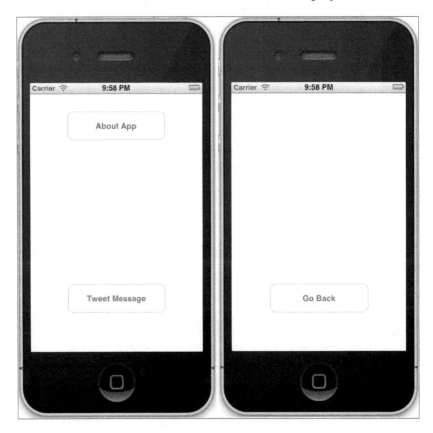

So there you have it. In this section, we have learned how to create and add new scenes into our main storyboard, as well as the process on how we are able to link-up and configure each scene when a button has been pressed.

There is also another way in which we can transition to scenes within our storyboard through a programmatic approach. We will be taking a closer look into this, when we embark on the section *Presenting storyboard view-controllers programmatically*, in this chapter.

Building a Twitter application

Twitter has provided us with some very simple API's to follow, making it a snap to interact with them. In this section, we will look at how we can use these to post a tweet message and add an image.

1. Open the `MainStoryboard.storyboard` file that is located inside the `TwitterExample` folder from the **Project Navigator**.

2. Next, drag a `UITextView` onto your view, and resize it to accommodate a reasonable amount of text to be entered, and make sure to delete the default text that is displayed within this control.

3. Lastly, we need to drag a `UIButton` on to the view to handle the posting of the message. In the button's attributes, change the text to read `Tweet Message`. Your final interface should look like this:

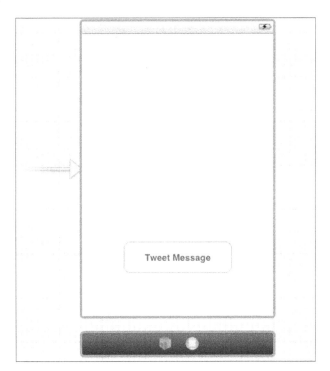

4. Next, open the `ViewController.h` interface file, and create the following highlighted entries as shown in the following code snippet:

```
#import <UIKit/UIKit.h>

@interface ViewController :UIViewController {
    UIButton *postTweet;
```

```
}

@property (nonatomic, retain) IBOutlet UIButton   *postTweet;
@end
```

5. Next, we need to connect up our **Tweet Message** button control, and create the `IBAction` event that will be used to post our tweet message. We will need to ensure that the type of event to use is the `TouchUpInside` method of the `UIButton`.

6. To create an action event, hold down the *Control* key on your keyboard, and drag the mouse to the `ViewController.h` interface file, as shown in the following screenshot.

7. Enter in `postTweet` for the name of the `IBAction` method to create, and then click on the `Connect` button to accept the changes.

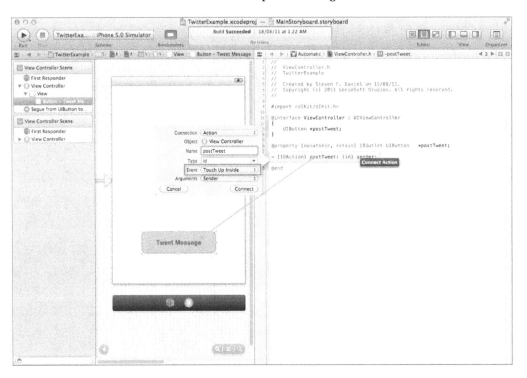

Now that we have connected up our IBAction event to our method call that will be used to post the tweet, our next step is to add the Twitter framework to our project before we can take a look at how to implement the code to do this.

To add the Twitter framework to your project, select the **Project Navigator Group**, and then follow these simple steps:

1. Select your project from within the **Project Navigator**.
2. Then, select your project target from under the **TARGETS** group.
3. Select the **Build Phases** tab.
4. Expand the **Link binary with Libraries** disclosure triangle.
5. Finally, use the **+** to add the library that you want. You can also search if you can't find the Twitter framework within the list.

If you are still confused as to how to go about adding the frameworks, follow this screenshot, which highlights the areas that you need to select:

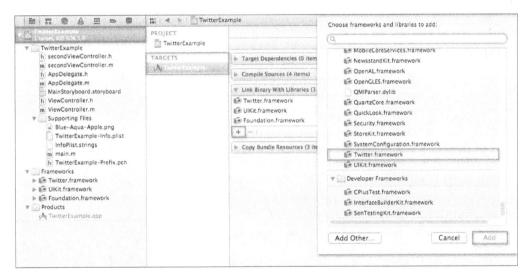

Now that we have added our Twitter.framework into our project, we can take a look at how to implement the code to post a tweet message using this framework.

Composing a Tweet message

Whenever you want to compose a Twitter message for submission, you will need to use the TWTweetComposeViewController class instance. This class handles everything required, and presents us with a tweet composition sheet, so that we can begin to type in our tweet message. This class also enables you to set the initial twitter text information to use, as well as how to go about adding images and URLs.

 For more information on the TWTweetComposeViewController class, you can refer to the Twitter framework reference documentation located at the following location: http://developer.apple.com/library/ios/#documentation/Twitter/Reference/TWTweetSheetViewControllerClassRef/Reference/Reference.html.

In the following code snippet, we look at how we can compose a Twitter message using the TWTweetComposeViewController class.

Before we can use the features of Twitter in our application, we need to include the Twitter framework header files.

1. From the **Project Navigator**, open the ViewController.m implementation file, and enter in the following import statements as shown:

```
#import <Twitter/Twitter.h>
#import <Twitter/TWTweetComposeViewController.h>
```

2. Next, we need to implement the code to display the Twitter tweet sheet to which we can compose, and then post our message. Open the ViewController.m implementation file, and enter in the following code snippet:

```
- (IBAction) postTweet: (id) sender {

  TWTweetComposeViewController *myTwitter =
    [[TWTweetComposeViewController alloc] init];
  [myTwitter setInitialText:@"Welcome to iOS 5 and Xcode 4.2,
    using the Twitter API."];
  [self presentModalViewController:myTwitter animated:YES];

  // Retrieve the result of the Twitter handler to
  // determine if the message was successfully sent.
  myTwitter.completionHandler =
    ^(TWTweetComposeViewControllerResult res){
    if (res == TWTweetComposeViewControllerResultDone) {
```

```
UIAlertView *alertView = [[UIAlertView alloc]
initWithTitle:@"Success" message:@"Your Tweet was posted
successfully." delegate:self  cancelButtonTitle:@"OK"
otherButtonTitles:nil];

[alertView show];
[self dismissModalViewControllerAnimated:YES];
}
else if (res ==
TWTweetComposeViewControllerResultCancelled) {
UIAlertView *alertView = [[UIAlertView alloc]
initWithTitle:@"Error" message:@"Your Tweet was not
posted." delegate:self cancelButtonTitle:@"OK"
otherButtonTitles:nil];
[alertView show];
[self dismissModalViewControllerAnimated:YES];
}
};
}
```

In this code snippet, we declared a variable `myTwitter` to be an instance of our `TWTweetComposeViewController` class. We then assigned some text to appear on our composition sheet, by setting the `setInitialText` method, and then displaying this to the view. We then set up a handler, using the `completionHandler` method, to notify us when the user has done composing the tweet, and we displayed the relevant alert based on the outcome that is returned by the method.

3. Optionally, you can use the `canSendTweet` class method to check if Twitter has been set up and is reachable, before presenting the view to the user. This is shown in the following code snippet:

```
BOOL isSUCCESS = TWTweetComposeViewController.canSendTweet;
if (isSUCCESS== YES){
  Do something...
}
// Twitter account credentials have not been set up correctly.
else{
  UIAlertView *alertView = [[UIAlertViewalloc]
    initWithTitle:@"Twitter Error" message:@"Your Twitter
    account has not been set up correctly." delegate:self
    cancelButtonTitle:@"OK" otherButtonTitles:nil];

  [alertView show];
}
```

What we have accomplished in this above code snippet is using the `canSendTweet` class method of the `TWTweetComposeViewController` class. This method then checks to see if the user has correctly installed and set up Twitter properly. If this has not been done, this statement will fail, and a value of `NO` (or `FALSE`) will be returned to the `isSuccess` variable.

Adding photos to a Tweet

Whenever you want to add images to a twitter message for submission, you will need to use the `TWTweetComposeViewController` class instance. This class handles everything required, and presents us with a tweet composition sheet, so that we can add images and URLs.

In the next code snippet, we look at how simple it is to add images to an existing Twitter message using the `TWTweetComposeViewController` class.

Open the `ViewController.m` implementation file located within the `TwitterExample` folder within the **Project Navigator**, locate the `postTweet` method, and enter in the following piece of highlighted code, shown as follows:

```
- (IBAction) postTweet: (id) sender {

  // Attach an image to our Tweet message
  TWTweetComposeViewController *myTwitter =
    [[TWTweetComposeViewControlleralloc] init];

    [myTwitter addImage:[UIImage imageNamed:@"Blue-Aqua-Apple.
  png"]];
  [self presentModalViewController:myTwitteranimated:YES];
}
```

In this code snippet, we declare a variable `myTwitter` to an instance of our `TWTweetComposeViewController` class. We then use the `addImageinstance` method to add an image to the tweet message, and then present the view along with the image to the user.

Now that we have added in the final piece of code to our `TwitterExample` application, we need to first configure our Twitter account information prior to building and running the application. Follow these steps to set up and configure Twitter.

1. Open the **Settings** application from the iOS home screen.

2. Select the **Twitter** option from the **Settings** menu.

3. Enter in your **User Name** and **Password** credential information, and click on the **Sign In** button. If you do not have a Twitter account, you can create one from this screen by selecting the **Create New Account** option.

4. Our final step is to compile, build, and run our `TwitterExample` application, by either clicking on the **Play** button within the Xcode IDE or *Command + R*.

The following screenshot shows our `TwitterExample` application when it is run on the iOS simulator.

When you start composing your tweet message, you can choose to have your current geographical location added to your message. This feature basically uses the Google Maps API to map the tweets and gives Twitter users the option of tweeting their location on `http://twitter.com/`, and then allowing others to view the precise location on Google Maps.

Attachments can also be added to the composed message, and this can be any valid image (PNG, JPG, and so on). Clicking on the **Send** button will submit the message to your Twitter account, and you will receive a message stating that the Tweet has been successfully posted.

The following screenshot displays the posted Twitter entry that was submitted by the previous screenshot, as it would look like when displayed on `http://twitter.com/`:

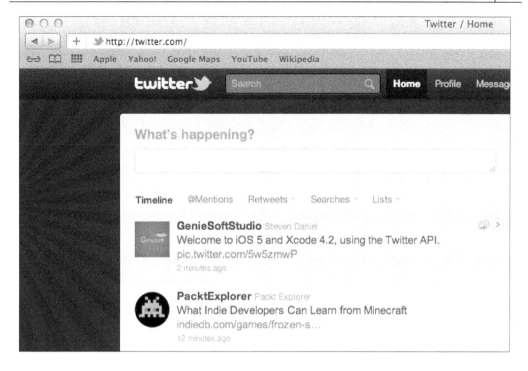

In this section, we looked at how we can integrate Twitter-like functionality into our applications. There are many ways in which applications can be more social, by including Twitter. For example, you could make the application auto-tweet, when you unlock a special item within your game, or when you finish the game, or just want to upload your high-score achievements.

This lets all of their friends know they are playing your game, which in turn, gets you more exposure. Another example could be a business application, which could allow the user to tweet the number of successful projects that they have completed. With Twitter getting so much attention lately, you would be crazy to not include some sort of Twitter integration into your own iOS applications.

Preparing to transition to a new view-controller

Whenever a user triggers a segue in the current scene, the storyboard runtime calls the `prepareForSegue:sender:` method for the current view controller. This method gives the current view controller an opportunity to pass any needed data to the view controller that is about to be displayed.

In order to programmatically perform a segue, follow these simple steps:

1. Ensure that you have drawn a segue between two the `UIViewControllers`.

2. Next, click on the segue and fill in the identifier field by using a unique name, as shown in the following screenshot:

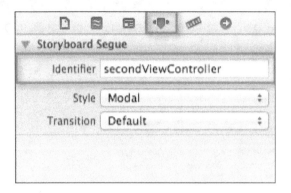

3. Now, run the `prepareForSegue:segue:sender:` method call from the `IBActionlevel` of the `UIButton`, as shown in the following code snippet:

```
- (void)prepareForSegue:(UIStoryboardSegue *)segue
  sender:(id)sender{
  // Check to see that we are processing the correct
  // segue, before processing the alert.
  if ([segue.identifierisEqualToString:
    @"secondViewController"]) {

    UIAlertView *alert = [[UIAlertView alloc]initWithTitle:
      @"TwitterExample" message:@"Currently displaying View
      #2" delegate:self cancelButtonTitle:@"OK"
      otherButtonTitles:nil];

    [alert show];
  }
}
```

In this code snippet, we perform a segue call associated with a control using its identifier. We first check to ensure that we are processing the correct segue, before displaying an alert when the view is displayed.

Handling it this way allows us to customize segues, and applies any transition to the scene that is located within your storyboard as long as the identifier is unique.

For information on how to implement the methods of the `UIViewController` class, you can refer to the `UIViewController` class reference at the following location: `http://developer. apple.com/library/ios/#documentation/UIKit/ Reference/UIViewController_Class/Reference/ Reference.html#//apple_ref/occ/cl/UIViewController`.

Presenting storyboard view-controllers programmatically

Although the storyboard runtime usually handles transitions between view controllers, you can also trigger segues programmatically, directly from within your code. You may choose to do this when setting up the segue from within Interface Builder, or you may want to use the accelerometer events to trigger a transition and display a graphic animation.

If you take a look at the following example code snippet, you will be able to see that we first load the view controller programmatically using the `instantiateViewControllerWithIdentifier` method of the `UIStoryboard`. Finally, we then present the view controller by pushing it onto the navigation stack.

```
// SampleViewController
- (void)viewDidLoad{
  [super viewDidLoad];

  // Instantiate the Samplesubview controller
  // from the storyboard.

  SampleViewController *subviewController = [self.mainStoryboard
    instantiateViewControllerWithIdentifier:@"subviewController"];

  // Note: the "subviewController" Identifier value must
  // be set in the Attributes Inspector on the
  // subviewController scene.

  // Add to self as child controller
  [self addChildViewController:subviewController];
  [self mainSubviewaddSubview:subviewController.view];
}
```

In this example, we will look at how we can add an additional view controller subclass to our storyboard, and programmatically determine what view we are in by using the `performSegueWithIdentifier` method call. So, lets get started.

We need to create a new `UIViewController` subclass file that will be used for our second view controller. To create a `UIViewController` subclass file, follow these simple steps:

1. From the **Xcode IDE** menu, select **File | New | New File...**.

2. Next, select the **UIViewController subclass** template to use from the list of available templates, as shown in the following screenshot.

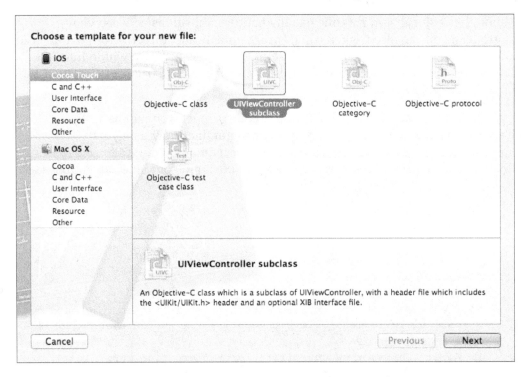

3. Enter in `secondViewController` as the name of the class to create, as shown in the following screenshot:

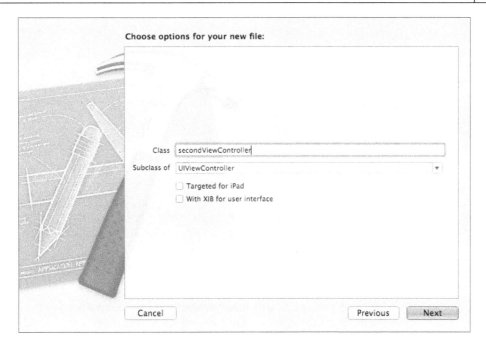

4. Ensure that you choose `UIViewController` as the name of the subclass to create.

5. Ensure that you have unchecked both the **Targeted for iPad** and **With XIB for user interface** checkboxes.

6. Specify the location to save the class file, and then click on the **Create** button.

   Once you have done that, you will be returned back to the Xcode IDE. Both of your interface and implementation files for the `secondViewController` will appear within the **Project Navigator** window.

7. Open the **ViewController.h** interface file, located under the `TwitterExample` folder, from within the **Project Navigator**.

8. Modify the file and include the highlighted code sections, as specified in the following code snippet:

```
//
//  ViewController.h
//  TwitterExample
//

#import <UIKit/UIKit.h>

@interface ViewController : UIViewController
  <UIActionSheetDelegate, UIAlertViewDelegate>{
```

```
    UIButton *postTweet;
    UIButton *aboutApp;
}


@property (nonatomic, retain) IBOutlet UIButton   *postTweet;
@property (nonatomic, retain) IBOutlet UIButton   *showAbout;



- (IBAction)postTweet:(id)sender;
- (IBAction)showAbout:(id)sender;



@end
```

In this code snippet, we are setting up our delegate objects in order to pass information to and from the view controller.

9. Open the ViewController.m implementation file located under the TwitterExample folder, from within the **Project Navigator**.

10. Modify the file, and include the highlighted code sections, as specified in the following code snippet:

```
- (void)prepareForSegue:(UIStoryboardSegue *)segue
  sender:(id)sender{
    // Check to see that we are processing the correct segue,
    //before processing the alert.
    if ([segue.identifierisEqualToString:
      @"firstViewController"]) {

      UIAlertView *alert = [[UIAlertView alloc]initWithTitle:
        @"TwitterExample" message:@"Currently displaying View
        #2" delegate:self cancelButtonTitle:@"OK"
        otherButtonTitles:nil];

      [alert show];
    }
}
```

What we are doing in this code snippet, is determining the current view of our view controller and ensuring that we are in our firstViewController. We do this by checking the segue property, and obtaining the identifier value that we declared previously. If we are in the correct view, a pop-up alert is then displayed to the current view.

1. Open the `secondViewController.h` interface file located under the `TwitterExample` folder, from within the **Project Navigator**.

2. Modify the file and include the highlighted code sections as specified in the following code snippet:

```
//
//   secondViewController.h
//   TwitterExample
//

#import <UIKit/UIKit.h>

@interface secondViewController :UIViewController
  <UIActionSheetDelegate, UIAlertViewDelegate>

- (IBAction)GoBack:(id)sender;            .

@property (strong, nonatomic) IBOutlet UIButton *GoBack;

@end
```

What we are doing in this code snippet, is setting up our delegate objects in order to pass information to and from the view controller.

3. Open the `secondViewController.m` implementation file located under the `TwitterExample` folder, from within the **Project Navigator**.

4. Modify the file, and include the highlighted code sections as specified in the following code snippet:

```
- (void)prepareForSegue:(UIStoryboardSegue *)segue
  sender:(id)sender{
  // Check to see that we are processing the correct segue,
  // before processing the alert.
  if ([segue.identifierisEqualToString:
    @"secondViewController"]) {

    UIAlertView *alert = [[UIAlertView alloc]initWithTitle:
      @"TwitterExample" message:@"Currently  displaying View
      #1" delegate:self cancelButtonTitle:@"OK"
      otherButtonTitles:nil];

    [alert show];
  }
}
```

Here we are determining the current view of our view controller, and ensuring that we are in our `secondViewController`. We do this by checking the segue property and obtain the identifier value that we declared previously. If we are in the correct view, a pop-up alert is then displayed to the current view.

5. Select the second view controller we just created, then under the identity inspector section, click on the **Custom Class** title bar, and change the **Class** to read `secondViewController` as shown in the following screenshot:

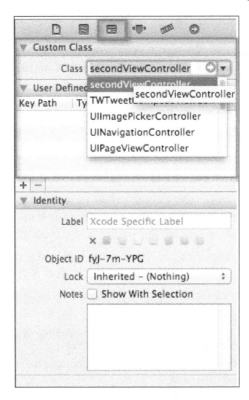

6. Under the attributes **Inspector** section, under the **Storyboard Segue** section, enter in secondViewController as the identifier to use when moving between views, as shown in the following screenshot:

7. Next, we need to apply the same Storyboard Segues for our first view controller.

8. Select the attributes **Inspector** section, and then under the **Storyboard Segue** section, enter in firstViewController as the unique identifier to use.

9. Repeat the same steps as we did for the secondViewController.

10. Our final step is to compile, build, and run our TwitterExample application, by either clicking on the **Play** button within the Xcode IDE or *Command + R*.

The following screenshot shows our `TwitterExample` application running within the iOS simulator, showing the programmatic transitions between each of the view controllers that are defined within our storyboard.

When you click on the **About App** button, it transitions over to the second view controller and then displays the message based on the `prepareForSegue:(UISto ryboardSegue*)segue` method call, determining the identifier of the current view controller that is being displayed within the view.

When you click on the **Go Back** button, this will transfer control over to the first view controller, a call is made to the `prepareForSegue` method, to determine the current identifier of the current view.

Summary

In this chapter, we learned the fundamentals of what storyboards actually are, how they work, how to go about adding scenes and configure these within the storyboard, and how to apply the different types of transition methods available.

We learnt about the Twitter framework and how we can use the collection of Twitter APIs available to successfully post a message and image to a twitter account. To end the chapter, we looked at how we can use the various methods to transition between each view controller within the main storyboard, programmatically, and using the storyboard transitions.

In the next chapter, we will learn about the **AirPlay** and **Core Image** frameworks, and look at how we use and implement these into our applications. We will learn about the different image filter effects and how to present these within our application to output this to an external device, such as Apple TV.

5
Using AirPlay and Core Image

Starting with the release of iOS 4.2, developers could use AirPlay to stream videos, audios, and photos to an Apple TV capable device. In iOS 5, it is now even easier to wirelessly mirror everything, automatically, on your iPad 2 to an HDTV through Apple TV.

With the additional set of APIs that come as a part of iOS 5, applications which are built using the AV Foundation framework now support encrypted audio and video streams, which are delivered through HTTP Live Streaming, and can also display different content on each of the HDTV and the iPad 2 screens.

The Core Image framework is a hardware-accelerated framework that provides an easy way to enhance photos and videos. This enables you to create amazing effects in your camera and image editing applications. **Core Image** provides several built-in filters, such as color effects, distortions, and transitions. It also includes advanced features, such as auto-enhance, red-eye reduction, and facial recognition.

In this chapter, we will be taking a closer look into what each of these frameworks are, and how to go about implementing these within our applications. We will take a look at how to incorporate AirPlay within our applications, and have this information directed to another output device using Apple TV. We will also be taking a look into the Core Image framework, and how to use the various filter effects using the `CIImage` class.

In this chapter, we will:

- Learn about the AirPlay and Core Image frameworks
- Create a simple AirPlay and Core Image application
- Learn how to output application content to an Apple TV device
- Take a look at how to apply various filter effects for distortions, transitions, and color effects, using the `CIImage` class

We have some fantastic stuff to cover in this chapter. So, let's get started.

Understanding the AirPlay framework

The AirPlay framework is an updated framework that lets you stream audio and video content from any iOS-based device to any Airplay-enabled device that is capable of playing audio and video, such as television sets and audio systems. Starting with iOS 5, developers now have the flexibility to incorporate Airplay content into their applications, and have this information presented out to a nearby Apple TV 2 receiver.

In this section, we will take a look at how to create a simple application to playback video content on an iOS device, and then take a look at the steps involved to output this to an Apple TV 2 device.

Creating a simple AirPlay application

Playing videos is one of the most common tasks that can be done on any iOS device, all videos must be played and displayed in full-screen. Before we can play any videos, we need to add the Media Player framework into our application project.

Before we can proceed, we first need to create our `AirPlayExample` project. To refresh your memory on how to go about creating a new project, you can refer to the section that we covered in *Chapter 1, What's New in iOS5*, under the section named *Creating the MyEmailApp application*.

1. Launch Xcode from the `/Xcode4/Applications` folder.
2. Choose **Create a new Xcode project**, or **File | New Project**.
3. Select the **Single View Application** template from the list of available templates.
4. Select **iPhone** from under the **Device Family** drop-down.
5. Click on the **Next** button to proceed to the next step in the wizard.

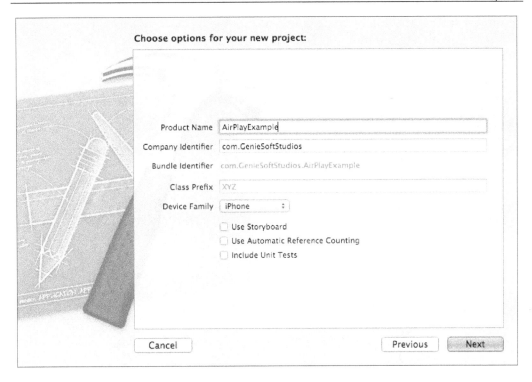

6. Enter in `AirPlayExample` as the name for your project, and then click on the **Next** button to proceed to the next step of the wizard.

7. Specify the location where you would like to save your project.

8. Click on the **Save** button to continue and display the Xcode workspace environment.

Now that we have created our `AirPlayExample` project, we now need to add an important framework to our project to enable our application with the ability to play movie files. To add the Media Player framework to your project, select the **Project Navigator Group**, and then follow these simple steps:

1. Click and select your project from the **Project Navigator**.

2. Then select your project target from under the **TARGETS** group.

3. Select the **Build Phases** tab.

4. Expand the **Link binary with Libraries disclosure** triangle.

5. Finally, use the **+** to add the library you want.

6. Select the **MediaPlayer.framework** from the list of available frameworks. You can also search if you can't find the framework you are after, from within the list.

If you are still confused how to go about adding the frameworks, follow this screenshot, which highlights the areas that you need to select (surrounded by a red rectangle):

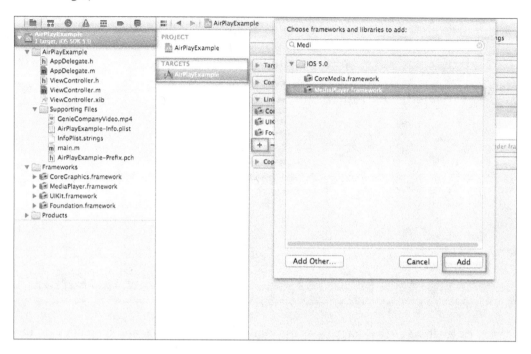

Now that you have added the `MediaPlayer.framework` into your project, we need to start building our user interface that will be responsible for playing the movie:

1. From the Project Navigator, select and open the **ViewController.xib** file.

2. From the **Object Library**, select and drag a (`UIButton`) Round Rect Button control, and add this to our view.

3. Resize accordingly, then modify the **Object Attributes** section of the Round Rect Button, and set its title to `Play Movie`.

We don't need to add a stop button, as we will be adding an event that will handle this for us when the movie has finished playing. If you have followed the steps correctly, your view should look something like that shown in the following screenshot. If it doesn't look quite the same as mine, feel free to adjust yours:

As you can see, our form doesn't do much at this stage, and if you were to run this application in the simulator, you would see the controls as placed out on your screen. The following steps will show you how to connect your buttons up to action events which will each perform the task of playing the video. So let's get started:

1. Open the `ViewController.h` interface file, and create the following highlighted entries as shown in the code snippet:

```
#import <UIKit/UIKit.h>
#import <MediaPlayer/MediaPlayer.h>

@interface ViewController : UIViewController

- (IBAction)playMovie:(id)sender;

@end
```

2. We need to create an action event. Select the **Play Movie** button, and hold down the Control key while you drag this into the `ViewController.m` implementation file class, as shown in the following screenshot:

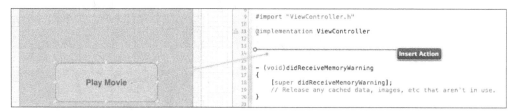

3. Specify a name for the action that you want to create. Enter in `playMovie` as the name of the action.

4. Set the type of event to be **Touch Up Inside**.

5. Click on the **Connect** button to have Xcode create the event.

6. We now need to add the code to our `playMovie` function which will handle playing our sample movie file. Enter in the following code snippet for this function:

```
-(IBAction)playMovie:(id)sender{

    NSString *filepath = [[NSBundle mainBundle]
        pathForResource:@"GenieCompanyVideo" ofType:@"mp4"];

    NSURL    *fileURL  = [NSURL fileURLWithPath:filepath];
    MPMoviePlayerController *moviePlayerController =
        [[MPMoviePlayerController alloc]initWithContentURL:fileURL];

    [[NSNotificationCenter defaultCenter]
        addObserver:self
        selector:@selector(moviePlaybackComplete:)
        name:MPMoviePlayerPlaybackDidFinishNotification
        object:moviePlayerController];
```

```
    [self.view addSubview:moviePlayerController.view];

    moviePlayerController.fullscreen = YES;
    moviePlayerController.scalingMode =
      MPMovieScalingModeAspectFit;

    [moviePlayerController play];
}
```

We have just declared a variable (NSString) filePath which will contain the file path to our movie file. Next, we create a (NSURL) fileUrl that converts our file path to an object, which is what the MPMoviePlayerController needs when it is being initialized. We then add the MPMoviePlayerController view to our custom view controller, so that it will appear on the screen. We specify that we want to display this full screen, and finally we tell the moviePlayerController to commence playback.

Since we have allocated memory to our moviePlayerController object, at this stage we haven't released it yet, this being due to not knowing when the movie playback will actually finish.

Fortunately, the MPMoviePlayerController object comes pre-built with methods to handle this scenario, and will dispatch a notification method called MPMoviePlayerPlaybackDidFinishNotification to the NSNotificationCenter when the movie playback completes, as shown in the highlighted code in the previous snippet.

When we playback video content within our iPhone applications, you will sometimes need to modify the scalingMode property of the MPMoviePlayerController object. By setting this property, it will determine how the movie image adapts to fill the playback size that you have defined. The following scaling modes currently exist, and are displayed here:

- MPMovieScalingModeNone
- MPMovieScalingModeAspectFit
- MPMovieScalingModeAspectFill
- MPMovieScalingModeFill

The two main common scaling modes used are the MPMovieScalingModeAspectFill and MPMovieScalingModeFill.

> For more information on the comparison between the different scaling modes, refer to the *MPMoviePlayerController Class Reference* at the following location `http://developer.apple.com/library/ios/#documentation/mediaplayer/reference/MPMoviePlayerController_Class/Reference/Reference.html#//apple_ref/doc/c_ref/MPMoviePlayerController`.

In order to implement this property in your application, insert the following line of code just before the [moviePlayerController play] statement:

```
moviePlayerController.scalingMode = MPMovieScalingModeFill;
```

When you run your application, you will notice that the video fills the entire available space. Next, we need to create the moviePlaybackComplete: method that will be responsible for releasing our moviePlayerController object, as shown in the following code snippet:

```
- (void)moviePlaybackComplete:(NSNotification *)notification{
  MPMoviePlayerController *moviePlayerController =
    [notification object];

  [[NSNotificationCenter defaultCenter]
    removeObserver:self
    name:MPMoviePlayerPlaybackDidFinishNotification
    object:moviePlayerController];

  [moviePlayerController.view removeFromSuperview];
    [moviePlayerController release];
}
```

In this code snippet, we passed an object to the notification method. This is whatever we have passed in the previous code snippet, due to the moviePlayerController object. We start by retrieving the object using the [notification object] statement, and then referencing it with the new MPMoviePlayerController pointer.

We then send a message back to the NSNotificationCenter method that removes the observer we previously registered within our playMovie function. We finally proceed with cleaning up our custom view controller from our display, and then release the memory we previously allocated to our moviePlayerController object.

The following screenshot shows our AirPlayExample application running within the iOS simulator with movie playback set up to be viewed in landscape mode; support is available to display this in portrait mode:

In this section, we learned about the `MediaPlayer` framework, and how we can use this within our applications to give us the ability to play audio and video.

As you can see, by using the Media Player framework and the `MPMoviePlayerController` class, you can incorporate movie playback within your iOS applications. In the next section, we will look at steps involved in modifying our application, so that this can be displayed on a TV screen using Apple TV. We learned about the various scaling modes for video playback and how to implement these.

Using AirPlay to present application content to Apple TV

Starting with iOS 4.3, Apple decided to provide its developers with one of the most impressive frameworks ever imagined, which would allow developers to integrate AirPlay features into their applications. With just a few lines of code, any iOS application can be modified to have the ability to stream video directly out to an Apple TV device.

To enable AirPlay functionality, we will need to enable a special property on our `MPMoviePlayerController` object, by setting the `allowsAirPlay` property to `YES`.

To enable AirPlay functionality within your application, follow these simple steps:

1. Open the `ViewController.m` implementation file that is located within the `AirPlayExample` folder, and locate the following statement within the `playMovie` function:

    ```
    [self.view addSubview:moviePlayerController.view];
    ```

2. Next, add the following code snippet:

    ```
    if([moviePlayerController
      respondsToSelector:@selector(setAllowsAirPlay:)]){
        [moviePlayerController setAllowsAirPlay:YES];
    }
    ```

    In this code snippet, we use the `.respondsToSelector:` method of the `MPMoviePlayerController` object to cater for older iOS devices that don't support the `allowsAirPlay` property.

    If we don't do this, it will cause a run-time error exception to occur which will crash your application. In order to offer AirPlay only to those devices that support it, we need to place a conditional statement around the statement which will check to see if the `MPMoviePlayerController` object supports the `allowsAirPlay` option.

[When this is set, it will cause an additional icon to appear within the movie player controller pane. You have no control, programmatically, over this icon placement.]

3. Finally, build and run your application, and click on the **Play Movie** button. The following screenshot shows what this icon looks like when AirPlay has been enabled:

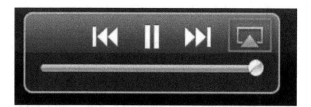

4. When the AirPlay icon has been pressed, you will be presented with a pop-up list of detected output device options to choose from.

5. If you choose the **Apple TV** option as shown in this screenshot, the output on your iOS device will disappear, and you will be notified that the video is being played on the Apple TV device. This is shown in the following screenshot:

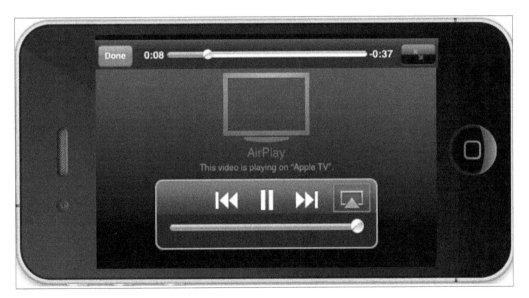

6. Finally, you will see your video being displayed on an Apple TV device, as shown in the following screenshot:

As you can see, by following a few simple steps, you can easily incorporate the functionality needed to turn your existing applications into Airplay-aware applications.

In the following list, you will find a few considerations to keep in mind when implementing AirPlay into your projects:

- Apple has only made this feature available on its most recent devices with the AirPlay 4.3 SDK. So, there is no AirPlay support for iPhone 3G devices.

- When launching an AirPlay-enabled application, you will need to ensure that both your iOS device and your Apple TV software are running the same version of the OS, otherwise you could run into some problems.

- In order for iOS devices to find other Apple AirPlay-enabled devices, you will need to ensure that you are on the same Wi-Fi network that your AirPlay devices are connected to.

For more information about the AirPlay framework, you can refer the following Apple Developer website: `http://developer.apple.com/` `library/ios/#releasenotes/General/WhatsNewIniPhoneOS/` `Articles/iOS4_3.html#//apple_ref/doc/uid/TP40010567-SW1.`

Understanding the Core Image framework

The Core Image framework is an extensible image processing technology architecture that has been built into Mac OS X v10.4 and iOS 5.0. This framework leverages the programmable graphics hardware to provide near real-time, pixel-accurate image processing of graphics, as well as video processing. The Core Image comes with over 100 built-in filters that are ready-to-use by filter clients who want to support image processing in their application.

The Core Image filter reference describes these filters; the list of built-in filters can change, so for that reason, Core Image provides you with the methods that let you query the system for these available filters. You can also load filters that third-party developers package as image units. The Core Image **Application Programming Interface (API)** is part of the **Quartz Core framework (QuartzCore.framework)**, and provides access to built-in image filters for both video and still images, and provides support for creating custom filters.

You can use the Core Image from the Cocoa and Carbon frameworks by linking to Core Image framework. By using the Core Image framework, you can perform the following types of operations, by using filters that are bundled in Core Image or that you or another developer create:

- Crop images and correct color, such as perform white point adjustment
- Apply color effects, such as sepia tone
- Blur or sharpen images
- Composite images and warp or transform the geometry of an image
- Generate color, checkerboard patterns, Gaussian gradients, and other pattern images
- Add transition effects to images or video
- Provide real-time color adjustment on video

The following screenshot provides you with a general idea of where Core Image fits with other graphics technologies in Mac OS X:

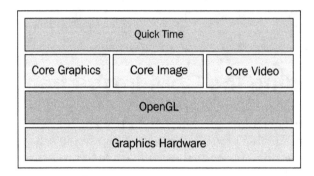

As you can see, the **Core Image** framework has been integrated with these technologies, allowing you to use them together to achieve a wide range of results. You can use Core Image to process images created in Quartz 2D (Core Graphics) and textures created in OpenGL. You can also apply Core Image filters to videos played using Core Video.

The Core Image comes with over 100 built-in filters ready-to-use by filter clients who want to support image processing in their application. The Core Image filter reference describes these filters; the list of built-in filters can change, so for that reason, Core Image provides you with the methods that let you query the system for these available filters. You can also load filters that third-party developers package as image units.

 For more information on the built-in filters that are available in the Core Image API, refer to the *Mac OS X Developer Library* at: *http:// developer.apple.com/library/mac/#documentation/graphicsimaging/reference/ CoreImageFilterReference/Reference/reference.html.*

The following code snippet displays a list of the available built-in Core Image filters.

```
NSArray *builtInFilterList =
  [CIFilter filterNamesInCategory:kCICategoryBuiltIn];
NSLog(@"%@", builtInFilterList);
```

The following table displays a list of available core image filters when this code is executed:

Core image filter name	Core image filter name
CIAdditionCompositing	CIAffineTransform
CICheckerboardGenerator	CIColorBlendMode
CIColorBurnBlendMode	CIColorControls
CIColorCube	CIColorDodgeBlendMode
CIColorInvert	CIColorMatrix
CIColorMonochrome	CIConstantColorGenerator
CICrop	CIDarkenBlendMode
CIDifferenceBlendMode	CIExclusionBlendMode
CIExposureAdjust	CIFalseColor
CIGammaAdjust	CIGaussianGradient
CIHardLightBlendMode	CIHighlightShadowAdjust
CIHueAdjust	CIHueBlendMode
CILightenBlendMode	CILinearGradient
CILuminosityBlendMode	CIMaximumCompositing
CIMinimumCompositing	CIMultiplyBlendMode
CIMultiplyCompositing	CIOverlayBlendMode
CIRadialGradient	CISaturationBlendMode
CIScreenBlendMode	CISepiaTone
CISoftLightBlendMode	CISourceAtopCompositing
CISourceInCompositing	CISourceOutCompositing
CISourceOverCompositing	CIStraightenFilter
CIStripesGenerator	CITemperatureAndTint
CIToneCurve	CIVibrance
CIVignette	CIWhitePointAdjust

The list displayed contains filters pertaining to both Mac OS X and iOS 5 operating systems, so it would be advisable to refer to the Core Image filter reference documentation to determine which filter applies to what technology.

 For more information on the Core Image framework and Core Image filter reference documentation, you can obtain these from the Apple Developer website at: http://developer.apple.com/library/ios/#documentation/GraphicsImaging/Conceptual/CoreImaging/ci_intro/ci_intro.html.

Creating a simple Core Image application

Apple provides more than 100 image-processing filters with Core Image, so it's easy for you to enable support for image processing within your application, using these built-in features. Image processing involves applying an effect to a photo to either flip or rotate an image, enhance the sharpness of an image, or even red eye from family photographs. Before we can do this, we need to include the Core Image framework as part of our application project.

Before we can proceed, we first need to create our `CIFilterEffects` project. To refresh your memory, you can refer to the section that we covered in *Chapter 1, What's New in iOS5*, under the section *Creating the MyEmailApp application*.

1. Launch Xcode from the `/Xcode4/Applications` folder.
2. Choose **Create a new Xcode project**, or **File | New Project**.
3. Select the **Single View Application** template from the list of available templates.
4. Select **iPhone** from under the **Device Family** drop-down.
5. Click on the **Next** button to proceed to the next step in the wizard.

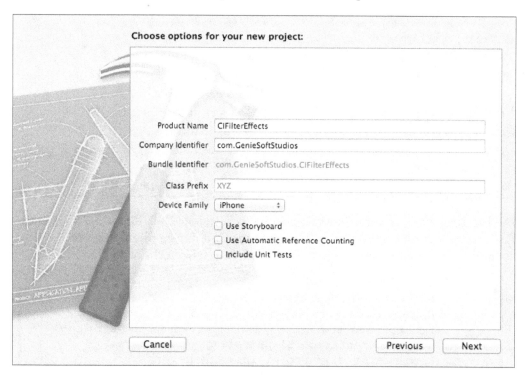

6. Enter in CIFilterEffects as the name for your project, and then click on the **Next** button to proceed to the next step of the wizard.

7. Specify the location where you would like to save your project.

8. Click on the **Save** button to continue and display the Xcode workspace environment.

Now that we have created our CIFilterEffects project, we now need to add an important framework to our project that will enable us to apply a number of different image effects. To add the Core Image framework to your project, select the **Project Navigator Group**, and then follow these simple steps:

1. Click and select your project from the **Project Navigator**.

2. Then select your project target from under the **TARGETS** group.

3 Select the **Build Phases** tab.

4. Expand the **Link binary with Libraries** disclosure triangle.

5. Use the **+** to add the library you want.

6. Select the **CoreImage.framework** from the list of available frameworks. You can also search if you can't find the framework you are after, from within the list.

If you are still confused as to how to go about adding the frameworks, take a look at this screenshot, which highlights the areas that you need to select (surrounded by a red rectangle):

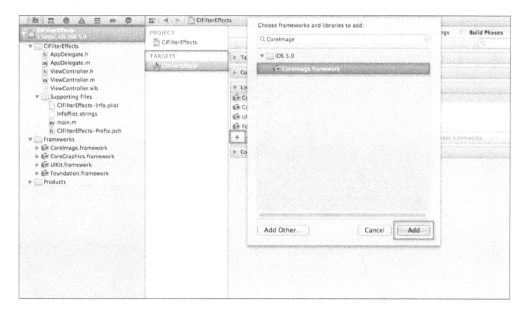

Now that you have added the **CoreImage.framework** into your project, we need to start building our user interface, which will be responsible for allowing the ability to choose an image and apply the filter effects:

1. From the Project Navigator, select and open the **ViewController.xib** file.

2. From the **Object Library**, select and drag the (UIImageView) image view control to our view.

3. Resize this control accordingly, so that it takes up the area of the screen.

4. From the **Object Library**, select and drag a (UIButton) Round Rect Button control to our view.

5. Resize accordingly and then modify the **Object** Attributes section of the Round Rect Button, and set its title to Choose Image.

6. Next, from the **Object Library**, select-and-drag a (UIButton) Round Rect Button control to our view to the right of the **Choose Image** button.

7. Resize accordingly, then modify the **Object Attributes** section of the Round Rect Button, and set its title to Filter Effects.

If you have followed the steps correctly, your view should look like something shown in the following screenshot. If it doesn't look quite the same as mine, feel free to adjust yours.

As you can see, our form doesn't do much at this stage, and if you were to run this application on the simulator, you would see the controls as placed out on your screen. The following steps will show you how to connect your buttons up to action events that will each perform the task of choosing an image, and apply the filter effects. So let's get started:

1. Open the `ViewController.h` interface file, and create the following highlighted entries as shown in the following code snippet:

```
#import <UIKit/UIKit.h>

@interface ViewController :
  UIViewController<UIImagePickerControllerDelegate,
  UINavigationControllerDelegate, UIAlertViewDelegate,
  UIActionSheetDelegate> {

  UIImageView *imageView;
  UIButton     *chooseImage;
  UIButton     *filterEffects;
}

@property (nonatomic, retain) IBOutlet UIImageView *imageView;
@property (nonatomic, retain) IBOutlet UIButton *chooseImage;
@property (nonatomic, retain) IBOutlet UIButton
  *filterEffects;

-(IBAction) getImage:(id) sender;
-(IBAction) getFilterEffects:(id) sender;

@end
```

2. We need to create an action event. Select the **Choose Image** button, and hold down the *Ctrl* key while you drag this into the `ViewController.m` implementation file class, as shown in the following screenshot:

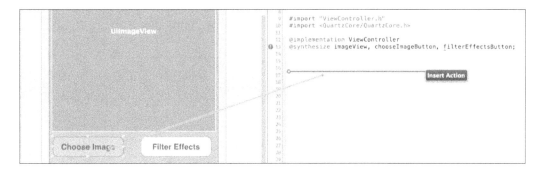

3. Specify a name for the action that you want to create. Enter in `getImage` as the name of the action.

4. Set the type of event to be **Touch Up Inside**:

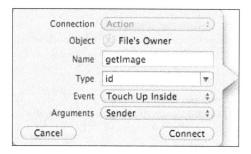

5. Click on the **Connect** button to have Xcode create the event.

6. We need to create an action event. Select the **Filter Effects** button, and hold down the *Ctrl* key while you drag this into the `ViewController.m` implementation file class, as shown in the following screenshot:

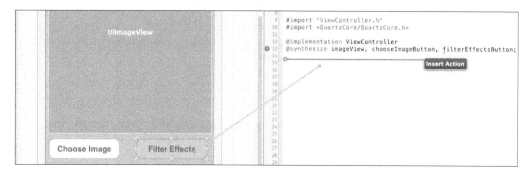

7. Specify a name for the action that you want to create. Enter in `getFilterEffects` as the name of the action.

8. Set the type of event to be **Touch Up Inside**:

9. Click on the **Connect** button to have Xcode create the event.

Now that we have connected up our action events, we now need to synthesize our user-interface controls so that we can access these within our view controller.

1. Open the `ViewController.m` implementation file that is located within the `CIFilterEffects` folder, and add the following highlighted statement underneath the `@implementation` statement.

```
#import "ViewController.h"
#import "QuartzCore/QuartzCore.h"


@implementation ViewController
@synthesize imageView, chooseImage, filterEffects;
```

In this code snippet, we are making our implementation file aware of the controls that are located on our user interface form. If these are not declared, we will receive warning messages, which could potentially cause your program to produce some weird results, or may even crash your application on the iOS device.

2. Next, we need to add the code into our `getImage` function that will enable us to select an image from the Photo library, and have this displayed into our `UIViewImage` control. Enter the following code snippet for this function:

```
-(IBAction) getImage:(id) sender {
  UIImagePickerController * picker = [[UIImagePickerController
    alloc] init];
  picker.delegate = self;
  picker.sourceType =
    UIImagePickerControllerSourceTypeSavedPhotosAlbum;
  [self presentModalViewController:picker animated:YES];
}

- (void)imagePickerController:(UIImagePickerController *)
  picker didFinishPickingMediaWithInfo:(NSDictionary *)info {
  [picker dismissModalViewControllerAnimated:YES];
  imageView.image = [info
    objectForKey:@"UIImagePickerControllerOriginalImage"];
  [picker release];
}
```

This code snippet creates an instance of the `UIImagePickerController` that will enable us to choose a photo image from the iOS devices photo album. We then modify and initialize the `sourceType` property of the picker control, and tell it to use the `UIImagePickerControllerSourceTypeSavedPhotosAlbum` constant. The final statement displays the photo album, and allows you to select an image.

3. We then declare another method, `imagePickerController:(UIImagePickerController *)picker didFinishPickingMediaWithInfo:(NSDictionary *)info`, that gets called after the image is chosen. The picker is then closed, and the image is then displayed into the `UIImageView` control, which we placed on our user interface. The `UIImagePickerController` class adopts the `UIImagePickerControllerDelegate` and the `UINavigationControllerDelegate` protocols.

4. Next, we need to add the code into our `getFilterEffects` function that will enable us to choose a filter effect from a list of options, and have this applied to our loaded image within the `imageView` control.

5. Enter in the following code snippet for this function:

```
// Displays our Action Sheet
- (IBAction)getFilterEffects:(id)sender {
    // Define an instance of our Action Sheet
    UIActionSheet *actionSheet;

    // Initialise our Action Sheet with options
    actionSheet=[[UIActionSheet alloc]initWithTitle:@"Available
      Actions" delegate:self cancelButtonTitle:@"Cancel"
      destructiveButtonTitle:@"Close" otherButtonTitles:
      @"Hue Adjust",@"Vibrance",@"Color Invert",@"Straighten
      Filter",@"Ripple Effect", nil];

    [actionSheet showInView:self.view];
    [actionSheet release];
}
```

This code snippet declares, creates, and initializes an `actionSheet` variable that sets up a list of filter options that can be chosen from, and then applied to an image. It is worth mentioning that the `UIActionSheet` class adopts the protocol `UIActionSheetDelegate`. The following screenshot shows you how these options will look when they are displayed:

6. Next, we need to create the `actionSheet` function that will handle and apply the required filter type to the image, based on the button index chosen within the list.

7. Enter in the following code snippet for this function:

```
// Delegate which handles the processing of the option buttons
//selected
- (void)actionSheet:(UIActionSheet *)actionSheet
  clickedButtonAtIndex:(NSInteger)buttonIndex{}
```

This code snippet will be used to determine what button has been selected from the action sheet options panel. This is derived by the `buttonIndex` property that is passed into this function. In the next section, we will look at how to apply these image effects, based on what has been chosen from within the list.

Learn how to apply image filter effects using the CIImage class

The Core Image class is used when you want to apply effects to images. These can be when you want to pixelate an image, or to handle red eye removal from your images. You can use the CIImage objects in conjunction with other Core Image classes, such as the CIFilter, CIContent, CIVector, and CIColor classes. In order to take advantage of the built-in Core Image filters when processing images, you can create CIImage objects with data supplied from a variety of sources, including Quartz 2D images and Core Video image buffers, using the CVImageBufferRef.

The CIImage object has image data associated with it, but it is not an image. A CIImage object has all the information necessary to produce an image, but Core Image doesn't actually render an image until it is told to do so. This method allows Core Image to operate as efficiently as possible. When using the CIImage class, this contains a number of parameters, which are explained in the following table:

CIImage class parameters	Description
Filter Category	This specifies the type of effect (blur, distortion, generator, and so forth) or its intended use (still images, video, non-square pixels, and so on). A filter can be a member of more than one category.
Display Name	This is the name that should be shown in the user interface
Filter Name	This is the name you use to access the filter programmatically.
Input Parameters	These can contain one or more input parameters that let you control how processing is done.
Attribute Class	Every input parameter that you create contains an attribute class that specifies its data type, such as NSNumber. An input parameter can optionally have other attributes, such as its default value, the allowable minimum and maximum values, the display name for the parameter, and any other attributes that are described in CIFilter.

If you take, for instance, the color monochrome filter, this contains three input parameters: the image to process, a monochrome color, and the color intensity. You supply the image and have the option to set a color and color intensity.

Most filters, including the color monochrome filter, have default values for each non-image input parameter. Core Image uses the default values to process your image, if you choose not to supply your own values for the input parameters. Filter attributes are stored as key-value pairs.

The **key** is a constant that identifies the attribute, and the **value** is the setting associated with the key. Core Image attribute values are typically one of the following data types:

- **Strings**: These are used for things, such as display names.
- **Floating-point numbers**: They are used to specify scalar values, such as intensity levels and radii.
- **Vectors**: They can have two, three, or four elements, each of which is a floating-point number. These are used to specify positions, areas, and color values.
- **Colors**: They specify color values and a color space to interpret the values in.
- **Images**: They are lightweight objects that specify images.
- **Transforms**: They specify an affine transformation to apply to an `image`. `CIContext`.

In the next section, we will take a look at how we can use some of these techniques when applying the various types of color effects to our `CIFilterEffects` application, when a filter type has been selected from our action sheet list of options.

Open the `ViewController.m` implementation file that is located within the `CIFilterEffects` folder, locate the
`- (void)actionSheet:(UIActionSheet *)actionSheet`
`   clickedButtonAtIndex:(NSInteger)buttonIndex`, and add the following code statement after the function declaration.

```
CIContext *context = [CIContext contextWithOptions:nil];
CIImage *cImage = [CIImage imageWithCGImage:[imageView.image
    CGImage]];
CIImage *result;
```

In this code snippet, we declare a `CIContext` variable context. This variable will be used for rendering the image object `cImage` to the view. We then declare a `cImage` variable object of type `CIImage`, which contains a pointer to the image within our `imageView`. Finally, we then declare a `CIImage result` variable that will be used to apply the image filter changes, and then output this modified image to the `imageView` control.

Color effects

In this section, we will look at applying each of the options displayed within our action sheet pop-up to our image of the Apple logo, which we have chosen from our iOS Photo library.

1. Open the `ViewController.m` implementation file that is located within the `CIFilterEffects` folder.

2. Next, locate the
   `- (void)actionSheet:(UIActionSheet *)actionSheet`
   `clickedButtonAtIndex:(NSInteger)buttonIndex,` and add the following code statement after the variable declarations that we applied in the previous code snippet:

```
// Handle when the Hue Adjust Filter option has been chosen.
if (buttonIndex == 1){
    CIFilter *hueAdjust = [CIFilter
      filterWithName:@"CIHueAdjust"];

    [hueAdjust setDefaults];
    [hueAdjust setValue: cImage forKey: @"inputImage"];
    [hueAdjust setValue: [NSNumber numberWithFloat: 2.094]
      forKey: @"inputAngle"];
    result = [hueAdjust valueForKey: @"outputImage"];
}
```

In this code snippet, we start by declaring a `CIFilter` variable called `hueAdjust`. This will be used to denote the type of filter that we want to apply to our image.

3. In the next step, we assign the variable `cImage` of type `CIImage`, which points to the chosen image within our `UIImageView` control, and assign this to be the `inputImage`.

Next, we assign the level of hue to apply to the image, by setting the value of the `inputAngle` property. Once we have done all of this, we then apply the `hue Adjustment` to the image, and return this to our `UIImage` result, based on the `outputImage` property, and then output this back to our `UIImageView` control.

 When setting the values of the `inputAngle` property, these have a starting range from a minimum value of `-3.14` to a maximum value of `3.14`. There is also a default value of `0.00`.

The following screenshot displays the image output with the Hue Saturation applied. You will notice that it changes the overall hue or tint of the source pixels:

Next, we will take a look at the **Vibrance** option and see what happens when this Core Image filter has been chosen from the list of options within our action sheet.

1. Open the `ViewController.m` implementation file that is located within the `CIFilterEffects` folder, and add the following code statement underneath the previous code block that we applied in the previous code snippet:

```
// Handle when the Vibrance Filter option has been chosen.
else if (buttonIndex == 2){
  CIFilter *vibrance = [CIFilter
    filterWithName:@"CIVibrance"];
  [vibrance setDefaults];
  [vibrance setValue: cImage forKey: @"inputImage"];
  [vibrance setValue: [NSNumber numberWithFloat: 1.00]
    forKey: @"inputAmount"];

  result = [vibrance valueForKey: @"outputImage"];
}
```

In this code snippet, we start by declaring a `CIFilter` variable called `vibrance`. This will be used to denote the type of filter we want to apply to our image.

2. In the next step, we assign the variable `cImage` of type `CIImage`, which points to the chosen image within our `UIImageView` control, and assign this to be the `inputImage`. Finally, we assign the level of saturation to apply to the image, by setting the value of the `inputAmount` property.

 When setting the values of the `inputAmount` property, these have a starting range from a minimum value of `-1.00` to a maximum value of `1.00`. There is also a default value of `0.00`.

The following screenshot displays the image output with the Vibrance saturation applied. You will notice that it reduces the image colors, while keeping a good balance of skin tones:

Next, we will take a look at the **Color Invert** option and see what happens when this Core Image filter has been chosen from the list of options within our actionsheet.

1. Open the ViewController.m implementation file that is located within the CIFilterEffects folder, and add the following code statement underneath the previous code block that we applied in the previous code snippet.

```
// Handle when the Color Invert option has been chosen.
else if (buttonIndex == 3){
  CIFilter *invert = [CIFilter
  filterWithName:@"CIColorInvert"];
  [invert setDefaults];
  [invert setValue: cImage forKey:@"inputImage"];
  result = [invert valueForKey:@"outputImage"];
}
```

In this code snippet, we start by declaring a CIFilter variable called invert. This will be used to denote the type of filter we want to apply to our image.

2. In the next step, we assign the variable cImage of type CIImage, which points to the chosen image within our UIImageView control, and assign this to be the inputImage.

The following screenshot displays the image output with the Color Invert filter applied. You will notice that the image colors have been inverted to show more of a negative image:

Next, we will take a look at the **Straighten Filter** option and see what happens when this Core Image filter has been chosen from the list of options within our actionsheet.

1. Open the `ViewController.m` implementation file that is located within the `CIFilterEffects` folder, and add the following code statement underneath the previous code block that we applied in the previous code snippet.

```
// Handle when the Straighten Filter option has been chosen.
else if (buttonIndex == 4){
   CIFilter *straightenFilter = [CIFilter
     filterWithName:@"CIStraightenFilter"];

   [straightenFilter setDefaults];
   [straightenFilter setValue: cImage forKey:@"inputImage"];
   [straightenFilter setValue: [NSNumber numberWithFloat:
     3.10] forKey: @"inputAngle"];
   result = [straightenFilter valueForKey:@"outputImage"];
}
```

   In this code snippet, we start by declaring a `CIFilter` variable called `straightenFilter`. This will be used to denote the type of filter we want to apply to our image.

2. In the next step, we assign the variable `cImage` of type `CIImage`, which points to the chosen image within our `UIImageView` control, and assign this to be the `inputImage`. Finally, we assign the angle level rotation to apply to the image, by setting the value of the `inputAngle` property.

When setting the values of the `inputAngle` property, these have a starting range from a minimum value of -3.14 to a maximum value of 3.14. There is also a default value of 0.00.

The following screenshot displays the image output with the Straighten filter applied. You will notice that it rotates the source image by the specified angle in radians. The image is then scaled and cropped, so that the rotated image fits within the view:

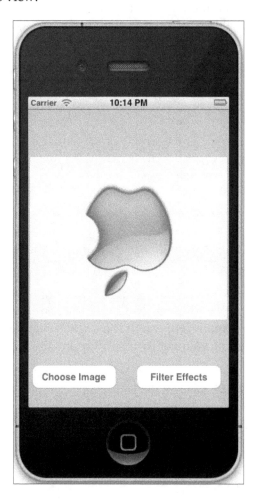

Next, we need to add the code that will be used to output the updated image once this has been applied based on our Core Image filters.

1. Open the `ViewController.m` implementation file that is located within the `CIFilterEffects` folder, and add the following code statement underneath the previous code block that we applied in the previous code snippet:

   ```
   // Only process when button index is based on the list of //
   options.Ignore the Close and Cancel buttons and then display
   // our update image to our UIImageView Control.
   ```

```
if (buttonIndex != 0 && buttonIndex != 5  && buttonIndex != 6) {
   self.imageView.image = [UIImage imageWithCGImage:[context
      createCGImage:result fromRect:CGRectMake(0, 0,
      self.imageView.image.size.width,
      self.imageView.image.size.height)]];
}
```

In this code snippet, we start by checking to ensure that we are not process-ing our **Close** and **Cancel** buttons, as those buttons do not apply the core im-age filters to the image. This is a general way of safeguarding our application to prevent it from crashing.

Next, we use the `imageWithCGImage` method to create and return an image object representing the specified Quartz image, then displaying this image back to our `UIImageView imageView` control, and setting it to be displayed to the width and height of the image view.

In the next section, we will take a look at how we can apply transition effects to an image while making use of the Quartz Core framework.

Transitions

Transitions are typically used to apply some sort of effect to an image. These effects are rendered over time and require that you set up a timer event. In this section, we will be adding some code to our `CIFilterEffects` example application to show one of the easiest ways in which we can apply a water ripple effect to an image.

Fortunately, you don't need to worry as there is already a ripple effect component that comes part of the QuartzCore framework, and this will take advantage of the graphics hardware acceleration when rendering this effect.

In order for us to start using transitions within our application, we will need to add an important framework to our project that will enable us to apply a number of different image effects.

To add the QuartzCore framework to your project, select the **Project Navigator Group**, and then follow these simple steps:

1. Click and select your project from the **Project Navigator**.
2. Then select your project target from under the **TARGETS** group.
3. Select the **Build Phases** tab.
4. Expand the **Link binary with Libraries** disclosure triangle.
5. Finally, use the **+** to add the library you want.

6. Select the **QuartzCore.framework** from the list of available frameworks. You can also search if you can't find the framework you are after, from within the list.

If you are still confused how to go about adding the frameworks, take a look at this screenshot, which highlights the areas that you need to select (surrounded by a rectangle):

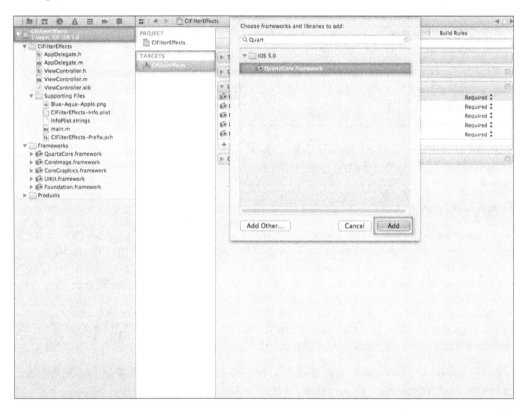

Now that we have added the QuartzCore.framework into your project, we can start to add the necessary code to our example project, to apply a water rippling effect.

1. Open the ViewController.m implementation file that is located within the CIFilterEffects folder, and add the following code statement underneath the Straighten filter code block:

```
else if (buttonIndex == 5){
    CATransition *animation = [CATransition animation];
    [animation setDelegate:self];
    [animation setDuration:3.0f];
    [animation setTimingFunction:UIViewAnimationCurveEaseInOut];
```

```
    [animation setType:@"rippleEffect" ];
    [self.view.layer addAnimation:animation forKey:NULL];
}
```

In this code snippet, we start by declaring a variable called `animation` that will be responsible for handling the transition animations for our `UIView` layer. In the next step, we specify the duration of our ripple effect that will be used to define how long, in seconds, a single iteration of an animation will take to display.

Next, we set up a timing function. This will be used to specify `UIViewAnimationCurveEaseInOut` as the type of animation that we want to use. This causes the animation to start off slowly, then accelerate through the middle of its duration, and then begin to slow-down towards the end of its iteration.

This is the default curve for most animations. In the next step, we specify that the type of animation we want to use is the `rippleEffect` transition effect. Finally, we then apply the animation effect to our view. The following screenshot displays the output with the water rippling effect applied. You will notice how it curves from the inside out, more like a vacuum effect:

As you can see, by using both the Core Image and QuartzCore frameworks, you can create some fantastic visual effects within your applications, and bring them to life.

> For more information on Core Image and the QuartzCore frameworks, please refer to the following link:
> `http://developer.apple.com/library/mac/#documentation/`
> `GraphicsImaging/Conceptual/CoreImaging/ci_intro/ci_`
> `intro.html`.
>
> For more information on the Core Image filters, please refer to the following link:
> `http://developer.apple.com/library/mac/#documentation/`
> `GraphicsImaging/Reference/CoreImageFilterReference/`
> `Reference/reference.html`.

Summary

In this chapter, we learned about the AirPlay and Core Image frameworks, and looked at how we can implement these into our applications to output them to an external device, such as Apple TV.

We then learned about the Core Image filters class, and how we can apply the different image filter effects to enhance images through the different built-in filters, such as color effects. We then familiarized ourselves with the QuartzCore framework, and looked at how we can use this framework, using the built-in filters for distortions and transition effects, to apply a water ripple effect to an image.

In the next chapter, we will learn about the improvements that have been made to the Xcode development tools, and take a look at **Automatic Reference Counting (ARC)**. This is the latest addition to the LLVM compiler. We will also be taking a look at improvements made to Interface Builder, the iOS Location simulator, and the set of debugging tools for OpenGL ES.

6
Xcode Tools - Improvements

Since the release of the iPhone 4 back in 2010, developers were impressed by the remarkable 960x640-resolution retina screen display, and provided a way to stay in touch with friends and family, using the FaceTime video-calling feature.

The iPhone 4 camera has been updated and features front and back cameras, as well as a standard 5-megapixel camera with a built-in LED flash and HD video editing that allows you to record and edit stunning HD video. With the release of the iPhone 4S, this has been updated to include the ability to record HD videos at 1080 pixels, with the added ability to directly edit your videos from within the iOS device.

Starting with Xcode 4, the **Gyroscope** feature was integrated into the Accelerometer, which provided developers the flexibility to program this and create some stunning games. With the release of iOS 5 SDK, the LLVM compiler has been updated to include the new **Automatic Reference Counting (ARC)** feature.

With the release of Xcode 4.2 and the iOS 5 SDK, Interface Builder has been updated to provide a better way of transitioning between your views and view controller, by introducing story boarding for your iOS applications, featured directly within the Xcode IDE.

You will also notice that the iOS simulator has also been revamped, and now allows you to simulate different locations using the Core Location framework, all directly from within the Xcode Development Environment.

In this chapter, we will:

- Learn about the latest improvements to the LLVM Compiler
- Learn how to create storyboard files using Interface Builder
- Learn about the changes made to the iOS simulator
- Learn about the improvements made to OpenGL ES
- Understand the application data management and UI automation enhancements

Let's get started.

LLVM compiler

This technology is an open source compiler technology, which is currently being led by Apple's compiler team to be used in several high-end performance projects around the globe. The LLVM 2.0 compiler has also been substantially updated, and now compiles twice as fast as the GCC compiler, producing applications that load faster on the iOS device.

It has been rewritten as a set of optimized code libraries, which have been designed around today's modern chip architectures. It has been fully integrated into the Xcode 4 development IDE, and provides complete support for the following languages: C, Objective-C, and C++.

In the next section, we will talk about the Automatic Reference Counting feature that has been added as part of the LLVM compiler.

Automatic Reference Counting (ARC)

Automatic Reference Counting (ARC) for Objective-C makes memory management the job of the compiler. When you enable ARC using the new Apple LLVM 3.0 compiler, this will largely remove the burden of manually releasing memory, and avoid the endless chore of tracking down program bugs caused by memory leaks or objects that have been released too early.

The ARC compiler has a complete understanding of your objects, and releases each object the instant it is no longer used, so applications run as fast as ever, with predictable, smooth performances. In a majority of situations, you will never need to type retain or release again, and this will dramatically simplify the development process, while reducing crashes and memory leaks.

Xcode comes with a new **Convert to Objective-C ARC...** tool, that is located within the **Edit | Refactor** menu within the IDE, as shown in the following screenshot:

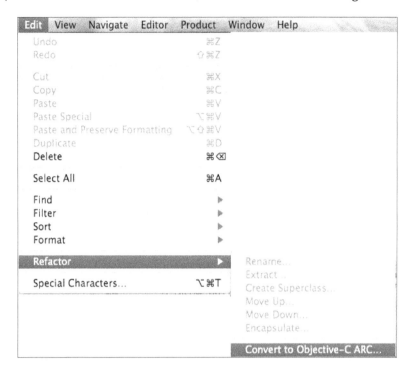

This tool automates the mechanical parts of the ARC conversion, by removing method calls such as `retain` and `release`, and helps you to fix issues the migrator can't handle automatically. The ARC migration tool converts all files within a project to use ARC; you also have the added option of choosing to use ARC on a per-file basis to overcome some of ARC's current restrictions, and use manual reference counting for some files.

The following screenshot implies that writing operative code takes almost as long to write as retain/release logic. This will not be true for experienced Objective-C developers, but if you are a new and just starting out with Objective-C, this is probably a conservative estimate.

> For more information on Objective-C, please refer to the *Apple Developer Documentation* at the following location: `http://developer.apple.com/library/mac/#documentation/Cocoa/Conceptual/ObjectiveC/Introduction/introObjectiveC.html#//apple_ref/doc/uid/TP30001163`.

You will still need to take some responsibility for how your classes manage reference to other objects, rather than relying totally on ARC.

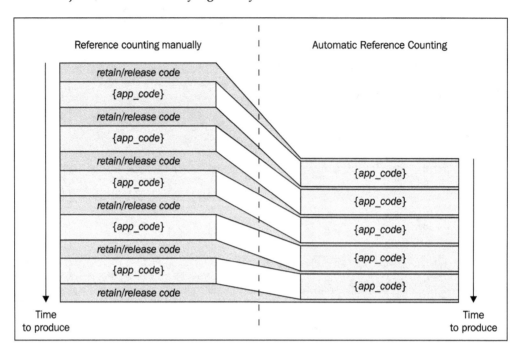

ARC provides automatic memory management for your objects, without you having to remember when to use retain, release, and auto-release. ARC starts by evaluating your objects, and automatically inserts the appropriate method calls for you at compile time, as well as generating the appropriate `dealloc` method calls for you.

For example, let's take a look at an example that shows the older way of doing things prior to the use of ARC, as shown in the following code snippet:

```
NSObject *obj = [[NSObject alloc] init];
...
...
// do some program logic here.
[obj release];
```

In between allocating and initializing an object, and then finally releasing the object, you can do with it as you wish, and the object will only be released and de-allocated when it is not in use.

Similarly, by adding the object to an auto-release pool, it will stick around until it is needed, and will be de-allocated sometime when it is no longer needed. This is shown in the following code snippet of how this would have been doing prior to ARC.

```
- (NSObject *) someMethod {
  NSObject *obj = [[[NSObject alloc] init] autorelease];
  return obj; // This will be released by the autorelease pool.
}
```

If you are new to iOS programming, you may have trouble getting your head around the use of reference counted memory at first, but once you get the hang of it, you'll soon see its potential. This is particularly useful when developing applications for iOS devices, as it can remove the burden of tracking bugs caused by leaking or over-released objects.

Many developers forget to release the allocation of memory to previously declared objects, resulting in sluggish performance issues, or more severe, causing their application to hang or crash.

Under ARC, this gets handled differently, and a pre-compilation step takes place, which adds retain, release, and auto-release statements into the code for you. This is by no means a form of garbage collection, and the referenced counted memory has not disappeared, it has simply been automated.

Take a look at the following ARC-enabled code snippet:

```
NSObject *obj = [NSObject alloc] init];
...
...
// do some program logic here.
```

The ARC pre-compilation step will automatically turn this into:

```
NSObject *obj = [NSObject alloc] init];
// do some program logic here.
[obj release]; // Added by ARC
```

In order for the compiler to generate the correct code, ARC imposes some strict restrictions on the methods that you can use, as well as introducing new lifetime qualifiers for object references and declared properties.

These new rules are not present when using the other compiler modes, and are intended to provide a fully reliable memory management model. They have been set up, in some cases, to enforce best practice. In other cases, they simplify your code so that you don't have to deal with memory management issues.

Violation of these rules will result in an immediate compile-time error, not some program bug that can become apparent at runtime. The following table explains the rules you need to abide by, in order to compile with ARC:

ARC rule	Description
Alloc/Init objects	When creating objects, you must not make any calls to retain, release, auto-release, and retain Count methods, or indirectly call their selectors, that is, @selector(retain) and @selector(release).
Dealloc methods	Generally these will be created for you, but you must not make a dealloc call directly. However, you can still create a custom dealloc method, if you need to release resources other than the instance variables. When creating a custom dealloc method, do not call the [super dealloc] method, as this will be done for you, and is enforced by the compiler.
Declared properties	Before ARC, we told the compiler how to memory-manage declared public properties using the assign, retain, and copy parameters using the @property directive. These parameters are no longer used in ARC. Instead, we have two new parameters, weak, and strong, that tell the compiler how we want our properties treated.
Object pointers in C structures	The Apple documentation suggests storing them in a class instead of a struct. This makes sense, since they would otherwise be unknown to ARC. It might cause some extra migration headaches.
Casual casting between id and void*	Casting between id and void* data types is frequently done when handing objects between Core Foundation's C library functions and Foundation Kit's Objective-C library methods. This is known as **Toll Free Bridging**. With ARC, you must provide hints/qualifiers to tell the compiler when CF objects are moving in and out of its control for memory management. These qualifiers include __bridge, __bridge_retain, and __bridge_transfer. You still need to call CFRetain and CFRelease to memory manage Core Foundation objects.

ARC rule	Description

`@autoreleasepool` instead of `NSAutoReleasePool`	If you use ARC compliant code within your applications, it must not use `NSAutoReleasePool` objects, instead it must use the `@autoreleasepool{}` blocks.
	
	A good example of this can be found within the `main.m` file of any ARC project.
	
	<pre>int main(int argc, char *argv[]){
	  @autoreleasepool {
	    return UIApplicationMain(argc, argv, nil,
	      NSStringFromClass([MyAppDelegate
	class]));
	  }
	}</pre>

Memory zones	You cannot use `NSZone` zone-based memory (This is not part of the runtime anymore); you cannot use `NSAllocateObject` or `NSDeallocateObject`.

As programmers, we find ourselves making decisions like whether to make something a variable or a constant, or whether or not it needs to be defined locally or globally. This same concept applies when we decide how our properties relate to other objects. To do this, we use the strong and/or weak qualifiers to notify the compiler of these relationships.

Strong references

These provide a reference to an object that stops it from being de-allocated. In other words, it creates an owner relationship. Prior to ARC, you would have declared your properties as follows:

```
// Non-ARC Compliant Declaration
@property(retain) NSObject *obj;
```

If we take a look at how this same property would be declared under ARC, this would be done as follows, to ensure that a class instance takes ownership of a referenced object:

```
// ARC Compliant Declaration
@property(strong) NSObject *obj;
```

Consider the following code snippet:

```
MyClass *obj1 = [[MyClass alloc] init];
MyClass *obj2 = obj1;
```

As you can see, we have declared two objects and have allocated the memory to our `obj1` object variable. We then declare a new object variable `obj2`, which has a strong reference to `obj1`. If we remove `obj2` from memory, then `obj1` also gets removed.

Weak references

These provide a reference to an object that does not stop it from being de-allocated. In other words, it does not create an owner relationship. Previously you would have done this:

```
// Non-ARC Compliant Declaration
@property(assign) NSObject *parentObj;
```

If we take a look at how this same property would be declared under ARC. This would be done as follows to ensure that you do not have ownership of the object that is being referenced.

```
// ARC Compliant Declaration
@property(weak) NSObject *parentObj;
```

Consider the following code snippet:

```
__weak NSString *weakName = self.textField.text;
```

We start by declaring a variable called `weakName`, which points at the same string object that the `textField.text` property points to - this contains the name `Albert Einstein`. If the string contents change, then the string object no longer has any owners and is de-allocated. This is shown below in the following piece of code:

```
__weak NSString *weakName = @"Captain Jack Sparrow";
```

When this happens, the value of `weakName` automatically becomes `nil`, and is what is called a zeroing weak pointer. This is extremely convenient, because it prevents weak pointers from pointing to de-allocated memory. Previously, this sort of thing used to cause a lot of programming bugs; for example, the term dangling pointers or zombies.

Weak pointers are mostly useful when two objects have a parent-child relationship. The parent will have a strong pointer to the child and therefore owns the child, but in order to prevent ownership cycles, the child only has a weak pointer back to the parent. Consider the following code snippet:

```
__weak NSString *str = [[NSString alloc] initWithFormat:@"Weakname:
%@",
    weakName];
NSLog(@"%@", str);  // This will output "(null)"
```

Since there is no owner for the string object (because `str` is weak), the object will be de-allocated immediately after it is created. Xcode will give a warning when you try to do this, because it's probably not what you intended to do (*Warning: assigning retained object to weak variable; object will be released after assignment*).

ARC qualifiers – regular variables

ARC introduces several new lifetime qualifiers for objects, and zeroing weak references. A weak reference does not extend the lifetime of the object that it points to. A zeroing weak reference, also known as a weak qualifier, instructs the compiler that you do not need to retain the object. If all the references to this object go down to zero, then the object is released and set to `nil`.

This is important, because a message sent to a `nil` object does not cause a crash; it simply doesn't do anything. However, you can still use `assign`, but it is recommended that you use `weak` instead, because it will set a de-allocated object to `nil`. A weak qualifier is especially used in a parent-child object relationship, where the parent has a strong reference to a child object, and the child object has a weak reference back to the parent, otherwise you will end up creating a circular reference.

Variable qualifiers

In the previous code snippets, we illustrated how our declared properties should be managed. For regular variables we have:

* `__strong`
* `__weak`
* `__unsafe_unretained`
* `__autoreleasing`

Generally speaking, these extra qualifiers need not be used very often. You might first encounter these qualifiers, and others, when using the migration tool. For new projects, however, you won't need them and will mostly use `strong`/`weak` with your declared properties.

ARC types	Description
__strong	This is the default, so you don't need to type it. This means any object created using `alloc`/`init` is retained for the lifetime of its current scope. The **current scope** usually means the braces in which the variable is declared (that is, a method, `for` loop, `if` block, and so on).
__weak	This means the object can be destroyed at any time. This is only useful if the object is somehow strongly referenced somewhere else. When destroyed, a variable with __weak is set to `nil`.
__unsafe_unretained	This is similar to the __weak type, but the pointer is not set to `nil` when the object is de-allocated. Instead the pointer is left pointing to an unsafe area of memory.
__autoreleasing	This is not to be confused with calling `autorelease` on an object, before returning it from a method. This is used for passing objects by reference, for example, when passing `NSError` objects by reference such as `[myObject perform OperationWithError:&tmp];`

For more information on the *LLVM Clang Objective-C Automatic Reference Counting* documentation, you can refer to the following link provided: `http://clang.llvm.org/docs/AutomaticReferenceCounting.html#ownership`.

Interface builder

In Xcode 4, the Interface Builder is a user interface design tool where you can build your user interface, by dragging and dropping objects from the Object Library onto a blank canvas. The resulting user interface would then be saved as an XIB file, which is an XML representation of your objects and their instance variables.

In the past, when creating a new view, you would have to create an XIB file for each view that your application required, to transition from each view to the next. In order to make designing your iOS applications much easier, Apple improved the user interface design process and introduced the **Storyboarding** feature.

Support for creating storyboard files for iOS applications

With the release of Xcode 4.2, Interface builder has been updated to provide a better way to design your user interfaces, by graphically arranging all of your views within a single canvas so that you can define your applications, logical flow as well as assign transitions between them.

Using storyboards within your applications, eases the development process by managing the view controllers for you. You can specify the transitions and segues that are used when switching between views, without having to code them by hand.

To refresh your memory, you can refer to *Chapter 4, Using Storyboards*, under the section *How to go about creating Storyboard files*, for more information on how to go about creating storyboard files using the Interface Builder.

Location simulator

Starting with the release of Xcode 4.2 and iOS 5, you now have the ability to test your location-based features in your application without leaving your desk. You can now select from preset locations and routes within the iOS simulator, and pick a custom latitude and longitude with accuracy, while you're running your simulated application.

Creating a simple geographical application

Before we can proceed, we first need to create our `MapKitExample` project. To refresh your memory, you can refer to the section named *Creating the MyEmailApp application*, in *Chapter 1, What's new in iOS5*.

1. Launch Xcode from the `/Xcode4/Applications` folder.
2. Choose **Create a new Xcode project**, or **File | New Project**.
3. Select the **Single View Application** template from the list of available templates.
4. Select **iPhone** from under the **Device Family** drop-down.

5. Ensure that you have checked the box for **Use Automatic Reference Counting** from under the **iPhone Device Family** drop-down.

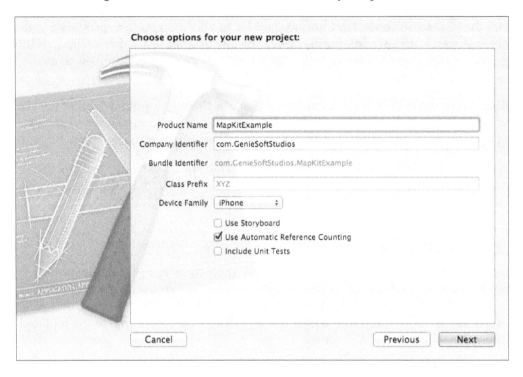

6. Click on the **Next** button to proceed to the next step in the wizard.

7. Enter in MapKitExample, and then click on the **Next** button to proceed to the next step of the wizard.

8. Specify the location where you would like to save your project.

9. Click on the **Save** button to continue and display the Xcode workspace environment.

Now that we have created our MapKitExample project, we need to add the MapKit framework to our project, in order for our application to view map information. Select the **Project Navigator Group**, and then follow these simple steps:

1. Select your project.

2. Then select your project target from under the TARGETS group.

3. Select the **Build Phases** tab.

4. Expand the **Link Library with Libraries** disclosure triangle.

5. Use the **+** to add the library that you want. You can also search, if you can't find the framework you are after, from within the list.

If you are still confused as to how to go about adding the frameworks, follow this screenshot, which highlights the areas that you need to select (surrounded by a red rectangle):

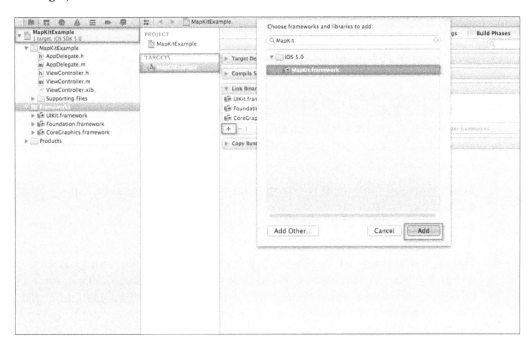

Now that you have added the `MapKit.framework` into your project, we need to import the code into the `ViewController` that will be responsible for displaying our map location information.

In order to make our application display the map to our view, we will need to import the `<MapKit/MapKit.h>` interface header file, so that we can utilize its methods:

1. Open the `ViewController.h` interface file located within the **Classes** folder, and add the following code:

```
#import <UIKit/UIKit.h>
#import <MapKit/MapKit.h>

@interface ViewController : UIViewController {
  MKMapView *mapView;
}
```

In this code snippet, we have included a reference to the Cocoa `MapKit.h` header file, which will expose its methods, so that we can use these within our `ViewController` implementation file, and then we have created an instance variable (`mapView`), which is a string pointer to our `MKMapView` object, which is responsible for holding our map location information.

2. We haven't quite finished yet. We now need to modify our `ViewDidLoad` method, located within our `ViewController.m` implementation file. So, open the `ViewController.m` implementation file.

3. Locate and uncomment the `ViewDidLoad` method, and add the following code snippet to it:

```
- (void)viewDidLoad {
    [super viewDidLoad];
    mapView = [[MKMapView alloc] initWithFrame:[self.view bounds]];
    [self.view addSubview:mapView];
}
```

In this code snippet, what we have actually done is allocated and initialized memory for our `mapView` object that we declared within our `ViewController.h` file, and then we added our `mapView` object to our current view, so that we can display this to the screen.

4. The `mapKit` framework has the ability to show you your current location within the map. It also allows you to set a variety of `mapTypes`. Next, we will be adding some additional code to our `ViewDidLoad` method as highlighted in the following code snippet. This is located within our `ViewController.m` implementation file.

```
- (void)viewDidLoad {
    [super viewDidLoad];
    mapView = [[MKMapView alloc] initWithFrame:[self.view bounds]];
    mapView.mapType=MKMapTypeHybrid;
    mapView.showsUserLocation=YES;
    [self.view addSubview:mapView];
}
```

In this code snippet, what we have done is added the ability to display our map in **Hybrid** view (combination of satellite view and road information) as well as directed our map to display our current location that will be indicated by an animated blue marker.

The iOS native maps application allows you to choose from the following three possible map types:

Map type constant	Description
MKMapTypeStandard	This is the default type of map to display, if none is specified, and this type will show a normal map containing street and road names.
MKMapTypeSatellite	Setting this type of map will display satellite view information.
MKMapTypeHybrid	This type of map will show a combination of a satellite view with road and street information overlaid.

If you build and run your application, you should now see a map displayed with the animated blue marker flashing. I have rotated the device and zoomed in at a random location to show the capabilities of the MapKit framework, as is shown in the following screenshot:

When running MapKit applications using the iOS Simulator, it will always default to Apple's headquarters located at 1, Infinite Loop, based out at California.

In order to get a better location, it is much better to use your iOS device. This is because the iOS simulator uses your IP address to work out an approximate location of where you are located.

You can also choose to navigate to a different location while the iOS simulator is running. To do this, follow these simple steps:

1. Click on **Simulate Location** icon as shown in the following screenshot. This will display a list of available locations:

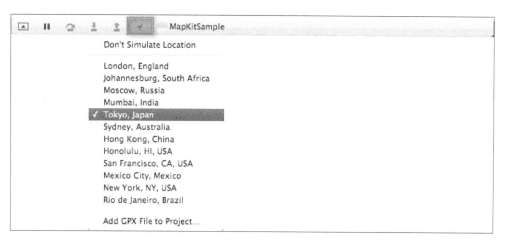

2. Select **Tokyo, Japan**, or a similar option from the list of displayed locations.

3. The iOS simulator will be updated to reflect the chosen location, as shown in the following screenshot:

In this section, we learned about the `MapKit` framework, and how we can use this within our application to simulate to a particular location. We learned how to use the **Simulate Location** feature of the Xcode debugger, to navigate to various locations within the iOS simulator.

 For more information on the `MKMapView` class reference, please refer to the *Apple Developer Documentation* at the following link location provided: `http://developer.apple.com/library/ios/#documentation/MapKit/Reference/MKMapView_Class/MKMapView/MKMapView.html#//apple_ref/doc/uid/TP40008205`.

OpenGL ES debugging

The OpenGL ES debugger allows you to track down issues specific to OpenGL ES within your application. You can then choose to have this break at a certain point within your program. To refresh your memory, you can refer to the section named *Detecting errors by setting up breakpoints*, that we covered in *Chapter 3, Debugging with OpenGL ES*, for more information on how to go about debugging OpenGL ES projects.

OpenGL ES frame capture

The OpenGL ES frame capture is part of the Xcode debugger, and allows you to take a snapshot of all of the frames that are being drawn within your application at the point it was captured. You can then choose to navigate through each of the frames and see the associated code, as well as changing between solid or wireframe view. To refresh your memory, you can refer to the section named *Breaking on frame boundaries*, in *Chapter 3, Debugging with OpenGL ES*, for more information on how to go about capturing OpenGL ES frames.

Application data management

iOS provides powerful connectivity options for sharing your information amongst the applications that are installed on an iOS device. Using a URL-based syntax, you can have your applications access data from the Web, as well as passing this information onto other applications that are installed, such as mail, iTunes, and YouTube.

Your own applications can declare a unique URL scheme, allowing any application to collaborate and share data with your application.

You can also choose to make use of XML files; these provide a lightweight structured format that your application can easily read and write. XML files readily fit into the iOS file system, and can be used to store your application settings and user preferences in the built-in **User Defaults** database. This XML-based data store includes a simple API with powerful features, including the ability to serialize and restore complex objects on demand.

For more information on the application data management feature, please refer to the following *Apple Developer Documentation* at the following location: DOCUMENTATION/DataManagement/Conceptual/ iPhoneCoreData01/Articles/01_StartingOut.html#//apple_ ref/doc/uid/TP40008305-CH105-SW2.

UI automation enhancements

The **Automation** instrument was added to the release of the iOS SDK 4.0. This tool allows you to automate user interface tests of your iOS applications, by scripting touch events, allowing you to log these results to be used for your analysis, later on. The Automation instrument comes complete with a script editor, so that you can choose to either write your test scripts to the UI Automation API using JavaScript, or load this into the editor from a file.

This is a huge leap forward for testing your applications on the iOS platform using test automation, which can reduce your time spent manually testing your applications. The Automation feature can be used to simulate many user actions on devices that support multitasking and, which are running iOS 4.0 or later.

You also have the ability to capture and record actions directly into your script as you perform them on an iOS device.

Automating UI tests allows you to:

- Free critical staff and resources for other work
- Perform more comprehensive testing
- Develop repeatable regression tests
- Minimize procedural errors
- Improve development cycle times for product updates

An important benefit of the Automation instrument is that you can use it with other instruments to perform sophisticated tests, such as tracking down memory leaks and isolating causes of performance problems.

> The Automation instrument does not allow you to process any application that is not code-signed with your provisioning profile, and this will not run within the iOS simulator. It needs to be run on an iOS-compatible device running iOS 4 or later.

Preparing your application

Before we can start to use the Automation tool, we need to do a little groundwork to prepare our application, so that it can work with the automation tool. The UI automation library relies on the accessibility information within your UI, so we will be adding this piece of information later, which will make testing of your application a lot easier.

Creating a simple UIAutomation application

Before we can proceed, we first need to create our UIAutomation project. To refresh your memory, you can refer to the section named *Creating the MyEmailApp application* in *Chapter 1, What's New in iOS5*.

1. Launch Xcode from the `/Xcode4/Applications` folder.
2. Choose **Create a new Xcode project**, or **File | New Project**.
3. Select the **Single View Application** template from the list of available templates.
4. Select **iPhone** from under the **Device Family** drop-down.

5. Ensure that you have checked the box for **Use Automatic Reference Counting**, from under the **Device Family** drop-down.

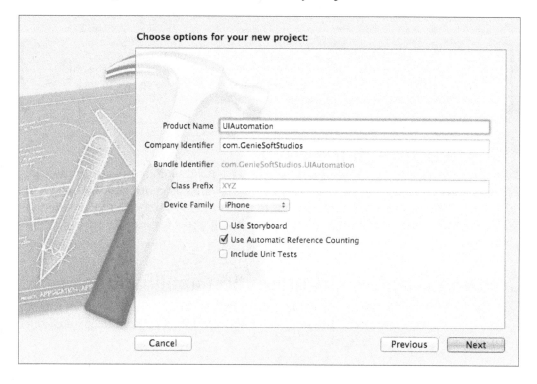

6. Click on the **Next** button to proceed to the next step in the wizard.

7. Enter in UIAutomation, and then click on the **Next** button to proceed to the next step of the wizard.

8. Specify the location where you would like to save your project.

9. Click on the **Save** button to continue and display the Xcode workspace environment.

Now that we have created our UIAutomation project, we can start to build our user interface, and add the required code.

1. From the **Project Navigator**, select and open the ViewController.xib file.

2. From the **Object Library**, select and drag a (UIButton) round rect button control, and add this to our view.

3. Resize accordingly, then modify the **Object Attributes** section of the round rect button, and set its title to Tap Me.

4. Next, from the **Object Library**, select and drag a (UIButton) round rect button control, and add this to our view underneath the **Tap Me** button.

5. Resize accordingly, then modify the **Object Attributes** section of the round rect button, and set its title to Press Me.

If you have followed these steps correctly, your view should look like something shown in the following screenshot. If it doesn't look quite the same as mine, feel free to adjust yours.

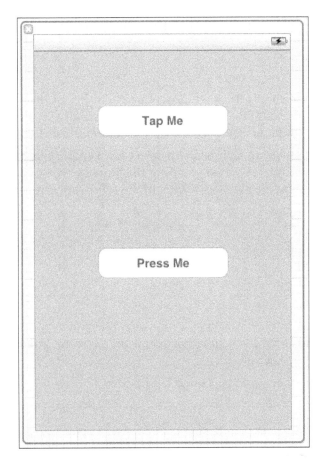

As you can see, our form doesn't do much at this stage, and if you were to run this application on the simulator, you would see the controls as placed out on your screen.

The following steps will show you how to connect your buttons up to their action events, so that can each perform their task. So let's get started.

1. Open the `ViewController.h` interface file, and create the following highlighted entries as shown in this code snippet:

```
#import <UIKit/UIKit.h>


@interface ViewController : UIViewController


@property (strong, nonatomic) IBOutlet UIButton *btnTapMe;
@property (strong, nonatomic) IBOutlet UIButton *btnPressMe;


@end
```

2. Open the **Assistant Editor** window, by selecting the **Open in Assistant Editor** option from the **Navigate** menu, or alternatively, by holding down **Option** + **Command** + **,** (Option key + Command key + Comma key).

3. We need to create an action event. Select the **Tap Me** button, and hold down the control key while you drag this into the `ViewController.m` implementation file class, as shown in the following screenshot:

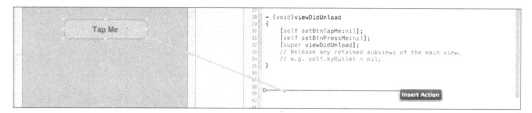

4. Specify a name for the action that you want to create. Enter in `btnTapMe` as the name of the action.

5. Set the type of event to be **Touch Up Inside**:

6. Click on the **Connect** button to have Xcode create the event.

7. We need to create an action event. Select the **Press Me** button, and hold down the Control key while you drag this into the `ViewController.m` implementation file class, as shown in the following screenshot:

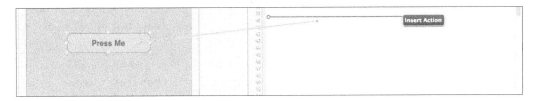

8. Specify a name for the action that you want to create. Enter in `btnPressMe` as the name of the action.

9. Set the type of event to be **Touch Up Inside**:

10. Click on the **Connect** button to have Xcode create the event.

Now that we have connected up our action events, we now need to synthesize our user-interface controls, so that we can access these within our view controller.

1. Open the `ViewController.m` implementation file that is located within the `CIFilterEffects` folder, and add the following highlighted statement underneath the `@implementation` statement.

```
//
//  ViewController.m
//  UIAutomation
//
//  Created by Steven F Daniel on 19/09/11.
//  Copyright (c) 2011 GenieSoft Studios. All rights reserved.
//

#import "ViewController.h"
```

```
@implementation ViewController
@synthesize btnTapMe, btnPressMe;
```

In this code snippet, we are making our implementation file aware of the controls that are located on our user interface form. If these are not declared, we will receive warning messages, which could potentially cause your program to produce some weird results, or may even crash your application on the iOS device.

2. Next, we need to add the code into our `btnTapMe` function that will be used to display an alert message pop-up when the button has been pressed. Enter in the following code snippet for this function:

```
// Event to handle when the Tap Me button has been pressed.
- (IBAction)btnTapMe:(id)sender {
  // Define our alert dialog popup
  UIAlertView *alert = [[UIAlertView
    alloc]initWithTitle:@"UIAutomation Example" message:@"Tap Me
    button pressed" delegate:self cancelButtonTitle:@"OK"
    otherButtonTitles:nil];

  // Display our alert
  [alert show];
}
```

This code snippet creates an instance of the `UIAlertView` class that will enable us to display an alert pop-up dialog box when the button has been pressed. You will notice that we have not released our alert object variable. This is mainly because ARC will be automatically managing the releasing of this object for us.

3. Next, we need to add the code into our `btnPressMe` function that will be used to help determine when the automation instrument has pressed it. Enter in the following commented-out code snippet for this function:

```
// Event to handle when the Press Me button has been pressed.
- (IBAction)btnPressMe:(id)sender {
  // Define our alert dialog popup
  // UIAlertView *alert = [[UIAlertView
    alloc]initWithTitle:@"UIAutomation Example"
    message:@"Press Me button pressed" delegate:self
    cancelButtonTitle:@"OK" otherButtonTitles:nil];

  // Display our alert
  //[alert show];
}
```

This code snippet creates an instance of the `UIAlertView` class that will help us determine when this has been pressed by the UI automation instrument, when we come to perform our unit testing. This code has been purposely commented out, so that we fail an automation test case that we will be setting up later on.

In the next section, we will look at how to set up our controls, so that they can be accessed and communicated by the Automation instrument. The UI Automation instrument library relies on accessibility information within your UI and looks for the `AccessibilityLabel` property of your controls.

1. From the `UIAutomation` example project navigator window, select the `ViewController.xib` file from the `UIAutomation` folder.

2. Click on the **Tap Me** button, and select the **Identity Inspector** button.

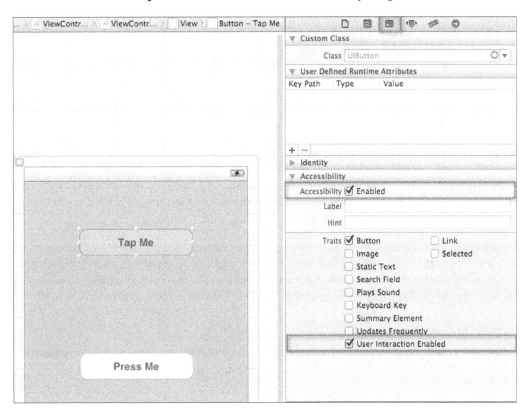

3. Ensure that the **Accessibility** option has been checked and that the **User Interaction Enabled** option has also been checked. This makes it easy to access only those objects that have these properties set, to be accessed directly from within the view. This is mainly due to their properties being exposed, making accessing these from within the UIAutomation test script easier.

4. Repeat *steps 2 to 3*, and apply the same to the **Press Me** button.

Writing the UIAutomation test script

The next step is to write the test script in JavaScript, using any editor of your choice. A **Test Script** is basically a set of ordered commands, each of which accesses a user interface element within your application to be used to perform some sort of user action on it, or to use the information associated within it.

All of the user interface elements within your application are represented to the script through an ordered hierarchical view of objects that are defined by the UIAElements class and its subclasses.

In order to reach a specified UI element, the script simply calls down the element hierarchy, starting from the top-level target object. The following code statement shows how to declare this in JavaScript:

```
var target = UIATarget.localTarget();
```

The UIATarget object is your primary starting point for your application running on an iOS device or iOS simulator. This object provides a means for when you want to interact with and when you need to perform operations on the iOS device, such as user gestures which include as tapping, swiping, and shaking.

The app object is an instance of the UIAApplication class that gives you access to the top-level structure of your application. This provides you with access to things such as tab bars, navigation bars, and the main window. The following code statement shows how to declare this in JavaScript:

```
var app = target.frontMostApp();
```

Now that you have an understanding of the UI elements structures, we can start to construct our UIAutomation test script. So, fire up your favorite editor, and let's begin.

1. Create a new blank document and save this as UIAutomation.js.

2. Next, we need to declare the objects to be used by our application. This is shown in the following code snippet:

```
// Initialise our application objects.
```

```
var target = UIATarget.localTarget();
var app = target.frontMostApp();
var window = app.mainWindow();
var view = window.elements()[0];
var buttons = window.buttons();
```

What we are doing in this code snippet is declaring a set of objects that we can use and make reference to within our code.

3. We have declared a target level object, which points to the top-level of our hierarchy, an `app` application object, as well as window, view, and buttons objects, which can be accessed from the `mainWindow` method.

4. Use of the `var` keyword tells the compiler that you want to declare a new variable instance of the object in memory. This is similar to the `Dim` (Dimension) keyword in Visual Basic.

5. Next, we want to add some initial header information to the results pane, to show which test case we are running this for, as shown within the following code snippet:

```
// UI Automation Test Case - Initial Logging
var testName = "UI Automation Test Case 1";
UIALogger.logStart(testName);
```

In this code snippet, we declare a variable `testName` using the `var` keyword, and then assign the automation header information. This information will be displayed within the results pane. Next, we use the `UIALogger` class method `logStart`. This tells the compiler to initiate the specified test.

6. In our next step, we need to determine how many buttons we have on our screen. This is shown in the following code snippet:

```
// TC001: Check for the number of buttons on screen.
UIALogger.logMessage("Assert Text - Check number of button(s) on
  screen");
if (buttons.length != 2) {
  UIALogger.logFail("FAIL: Invalid number of button(s)");
}
else {
  UIALogger.logPass("PASS: Correct number of button(s)");
}
```

In this code snippet, we use the `logMessage` method to log the message to the results window. We then use the buttons object to determine how many buttons are visible within our view, and then handle this using the `logFail` and `logPass` methods.

The `logFail` method logs the message to the results pane, indicating that the test completed unsuccessfully. The `logPass` method logs the message to the results pane, indicating that the test completed successfully.

7. In the next step, there may be times when you want to check if a specific button has been pressed. This is shown in the following code snippet:

```
// TC002: Check for the existence of the Press Me
// button within the view.
UIALogger.logMessage("Assert Text - Check for the existence of the
  Press Me button.");

// Get a handle to the button that we are after.
var btnPressMe = buttons.firstWithName("Press Me");
if (btnPressMe == null || btnPressMe.toString() == "[object
  UIAElementNil]") {
  UIALogger.logFail("FAIL: Press Me button not found.");
}

else {
  UIALogger.logPass("PASS: Press Me button was found.");
}
```

In this code snippet, we use the `firstWithName` method of the `UIAElementArray` class to return the first element in the buttons array with the name of `Press Me`. We then compare and check if the button exists, by using the `null` and `UIAElementNil` objects, to prevent it from raising an exception error, before finally using the `logFail` and `logPass` methods of the `UIALogger` class to output the result of the test to the results pane.

8. In the next step, there may be times when you want to simulate a tap for a particular button that is displayed on the screen, and have an alert pop-up displayed. This is shown in the following code snippet:

```
// TC003: Tap on the Press Me button and check for the alert.
UIALogger.logMessage("Assert Text - Checking for the Press Me
  Alert dialog.");
var btnPressMe = buttons.firstWithName("Press Me");

// Simulate a tap on the Press Me button
btnPressMe.tap();

var alert = app.alert();
if (alert == null || alert.toString() == "[object UIAElementNil]")
{
```

```
    UIALogger.logFail("FAIL: The alert dialog was not shown after
      pressing the button.");
  }
  else {
    UIALogger.logPass("PASS: The alert dialog was shown after
      pressing the button.");
  }
```

In this code snippet, we use the `firstWithName` method of the `UIElemen-tArray` class to return the first element in the buttons array with the name of `Press Me`. We then use the `tap` method of the button to simulate a tap. When this happens, the associated code that is connected behind the button is executed, and an alert is displayed.

We then declare an `alert` variable that takes on the alert `UIAAlert` object, returned by the `app` object representing the alert. Next, we compare and check if the alert exists by using the `null` and `UIAElementNil` objects to catch the error, preventing it from raising an `exception` error. Finally, we output the result returned to the results pane, using the `logFail` and `logPass` methods of the `UIALogger` class.

9. In our final part, we want to display to the results pane that our test case has completed. This is shown in the following code snippet:

```
// UI Automation Test Case 1 Completed
UIALogger.logMessage("UI Automation Test Case 1 Completed. Please
  check results panel for any errors.");
```

In this code snippet, we use the `logMessage` method to log the message to the results window to show that the UI automation test case has completed, or a process can be used to click the button on the alert dialog box, after the delay has completed.

The following table displays all methods pertaining to the `UIALogger` class. It has been broken up into sections to highlight which ones are used for logging status, and which ones can be used to specify the type of severity.

Logging with test status	
`logStart`	Logs a message, and indicates a test has started
`logPass`	Logs a message, and indicates a test has completed successfully
`logIssue`	Logs a message, and indicates a test has terminated abnormally
`logFail`	Logs a message, and indicates a test has failed
Logging with severity levels	
`logDebug`	Logs the specified message, and sets the severity level to `debug`
`logMessage`	Logs the specified message, and sets the severity level to `message`
`logWarning`	Logs the specified message, and sets the severity level to `warning`
`logError`	Logs the specified message, and sets the severity level to `error`

For more information on the UI automation class reference and the JavaScript API, you can refer to *Apple Developer Documentation* at the following link: `http://developer.apple.com/library/ios/#documentation/DeveloperTools/Reference/UIAuto/_index.html`.

Now that we have created our test script, we are ready to tackle the next part, where we start to profile our `UIAutomation` example application. This is covered in the next section *Running your tests*.

Running your tests

Now that we have created our tests, our next step is to profile our `UIAutomation` example application, within the Instruments application environment.

1. Launch Xcode from the `/Xcode4/Applications` folder.

2. Open the `UIAutomation` project, or **File | Open...**.

3. Choose **Profile** from the **Product | Profile** menu, or *Command + I*.

4. This will launch the **Xcode Instruments** application. Choose **Automation** from the iOS templates section, as shown in the following screenshot:

5. Next, click on the **Profile** button to proceed to the next step.

6. From the **Instruments** window, click on the **Add** button, and choose **Import...** from the drop-down list, as shown in the following screenshot:

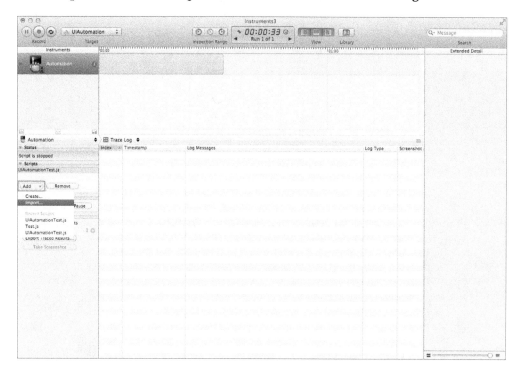

7. Next, choose the `UIAutomationTest.js` file from the list, and click on the **Open** button to load this file into the Instruments application.

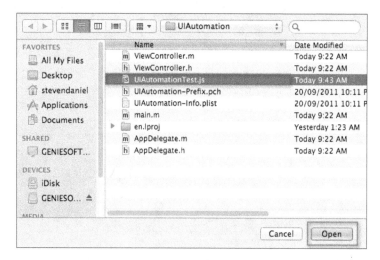

8. Finally, click on the **Record** button, or *Command + R* to begin profiling the `UIAutomation` example application. After a few moments, your application will launch and then your tests will run. This is shown in the following screenshot:

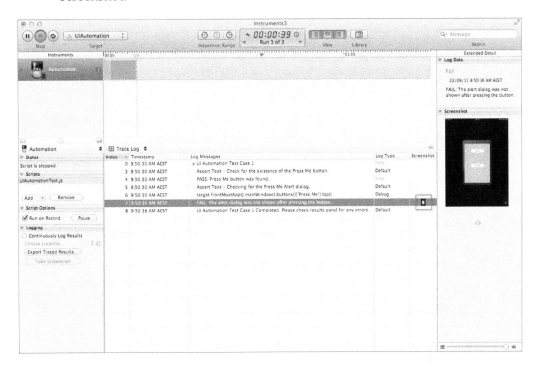

9. Once your test completes, the instruments application will continue to run your application. To formally end the test being executed, click on the red **Stop** button, or press *Command + R* again.

Test results are listed in the details view section, along with the test name in the **Log Messages** column. If you test passes, the **Log Type** column value will be **Pass**, shown in green. If your test fails, the **Log Type** value will be **Fail**, shown in red.

You can choose to expand the test results to see the details of what happened. The screenshot column is used whenever a test fails. In our case, no alert dialog box was displayed, and so, a screenshot was captured to show that it failed. This is shown in the following screenshot:

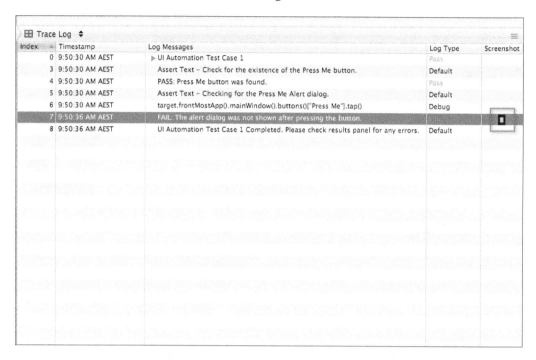

10. Go back to the `UIAutomation` example project, and uncomment the `alert` pop-up dialog code within the `btnPressMe` event, as shown in the following code snippet:

```
// Event to handle when the Press Me button has been pressed.
  - (IBAction)btnPressMe:(id)sender {
  // Define our alert dialog popup
  UIAlertView *alert = [[UIAlertView
    alloc]initWithTitle:@"UIAutomation Example" message:@"Press Me
    button pressed" delegate:self cancelButtonTitle:@"OK"
    otherButtonTitles:nil];

  // Display our alert
  [alert show];
}
```

11. Now, compile and re-run the test again. We should now see that within the details view section and under the **Log Messages** column, all of our tests should now be showing with the value **Pass**, shown in green. This is shown in the following screenshot:

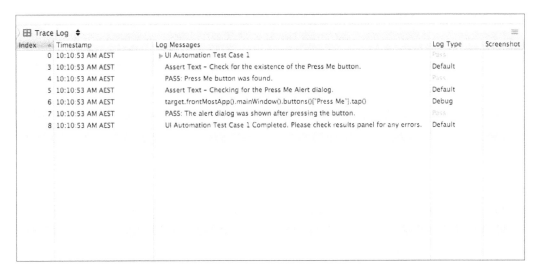

As you can see, by including the `UIAutomation` instrument as part of your testing, you can halve your testing time and concentrate more on fixing up those annoying program bugs, prior to your application being released.

Summary

In this chapter, we learned about the improvements that have been made to the Xcode development tools. We gained an understanding of what the **Automatic Reference Counting (ARC)** is, and some of the coding differences that need to be applied.

We also looked at the improvements made to Interface Builder, the iOS location simulator, and the set of debugging tools for OpenGL ES. To end the chapter, we looked at how we can use the automation instrument to help perform unit testing on an application, using a test script written using JavaScript to the UI automation API.

In our final chapter, we will be taking a look into how to go about making your applications run smoothly, at the new features that come with Instruments, and how to use these to track improve your applications performance.

7
Making your Applications Run Smoothly using Instruments

Well done for making it to the final chapter of this book. In this chapter, we will focus on how we can effectively use **Instruments** within our applications to track down areas within our iOS applications that could be affecting the overall performance.

These types of issues could potentially cause our applications to run slowly or even crash on the user's iOS device. We will take a look into each of the different types of built-in instruments, which come as a part of the Instruments application, and how we can use the **System Trace** for iOS instruments to help you track down system calls, memory, and threads within your code that may be affecting the application's performance on your iOS applications.

We then take a look at how we can configure instruments to display data differently within the trace document that is being reported.

In this chapter, we will be covering the following topics:

- Introducing the Instruments environment
- Learning how to add and profile against different instrument sets
- Learning how to check performance of your iOS applications
- Introducing other components of the Instruments family
- Introducing the new Instruments included with Xcode 4.2

We have got quite a bit to cover. So, let's get started.

Introduction to Instruments

The Instruments application is a powerful tool that enables you to collect information about the performance of your application over time. Through the use of the Instruments application, you can gather information based on a variety of different types of data, and view them side-by-side at the same time. This will therefore allow you to spot trends which would be hard to spot otherwise, and this can be used to see code running by your program along with the corresponding memory usage.

The Instruments application comes with a standard library, which you can use to examine various aspects of your code. You can configure Instruments to gather data about the same process or about different processes on the system.

Each instrument collects and displays different types of information relating to file access, memory usage, Network connections, and so on. The following screenshot shows the Instruments application profiling our `MapKitExample`, using a number of different types of instruments to monitor the system behavior:

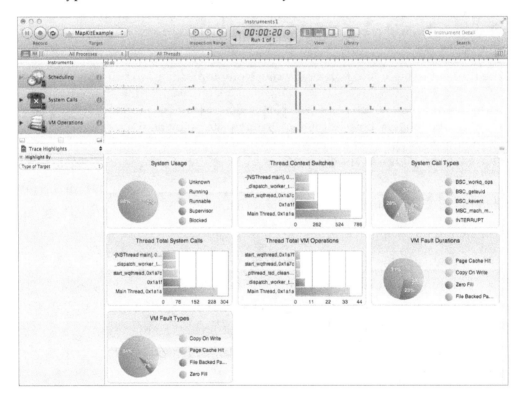

The following information in the table outlines each feature of the Instruments application, and provides a description about what each part covers:

Instruments feature	Description
Instruments Pane	This section lists all of the instruments, which have been added for those that you want to profile against. New instruments can be added by selecting and then dragging each one from the instruments library into this pane. Items within this pane can also be deleted.
Track Pane	This section displays a graphical summary of the data returned by the current instruments. Each instrument has its own track, which provides a chart of the data that is collected by that instrument. The information within this pane is read-only.
Detail Pane	This section shows the details of the data collected by each of the instruments. It displays the set of events gathered and used to create the graphical view in the track pane. Depending on the type of instrument, information that is represented within this pane can be customized to represent the data differently.
Extended Detail Pane	This section shows you detailed information about the item that is currently selected in the Detail pane. This pane displays the complete stack trace, timestamp, and other instrument-specific data gathered for the given event.
Navigation Bar	This shows you where you are, and the steps you took to get there. It includes two menus – the active instrument menu and the detail view menu. You can click on the entries within the navigation bar to select the active instrument, and the level and type of information in the detail view.

The Instruments trace document toolbar allows you to add and control instruments, open view, and configure the track pane.

The following table provides an explanation for each of the different controls on the toolbar:

Toolbar item	Description
Pause/Resume button	Pauses the gathering of trace data during a recording. Selecting this option does not actually stop the recording; it just simply stops the instruments from gathering data while a recording is in progress. When the **Pause** button has been pressed, in the track pane it will show a gap in the trace data to highlight this.
Record/Stop button	Starts or stops the recording process. You use this button to begin gathering trace data for your application.
Loop button	Enables you to set whether the recorder should loop during playback, to repeat the recorded steps continuously. This can be useful if you want to gather multiple runs for a given set of steps.
Target menu	Selects the trace target for the document. This is the process for which data is gathered.
Inspection Range control	This enables you to select a time range in the track pane. When this has been set, the instrument displays only the data collected within the specified time period. Using the buttons with this control enable you to set the start and end points of the inspection range, and to clear the current range.
Time/Run control	Shows the time elapsed by the current document trace. If the trace document contains multiple data runs associated with it, you can use the arrow controls to choose which run data you want to display in the track pane.
View control	Hides or shows the Instruments pane, Detail pane, and Extended View pane. This control makes it easier to only focus on the area in which you are interested in.
Library button	Hides or shows the instrument library window.
Search field	This option filters information within the Detail pane, based on a search term that you enter.

The Instruments application comes part of the Xcode 4 Tools installation, and can be found located within the `<Root>/Developer/Applications` folder, where `<Root>` is the installation folder where Xcode 4 is installed on your system.

Tracing iOS applications

One common use for Instruments is the performance of a system trace on your application. This nifty new Instrument, which has been added to the release of Xcode 4.2, helps you track down system calls, memory, and threads which may be affecting application performance on your iOS applications.

To show the use of the System Trace for iOS Instruments, we will use the MapKitExample that we created back in *Chapter 6, Xcode Tools – Improvements*. There are many ways in which you can start the instruments application; you can run Instruments and then have it launch the iOS application, or you can use the tools under the **Product** menu from within Xcode. The next section shows you how to run and profilie theMapKitExample application project.

Loading the MapKitExample project

Before we proceed to profile our MapKitExample project, we must first launch the Xcode development environment. This can be located in the /Xcode4/Applications folder. Alternatively, you can use spotlight to search for Xcode, by typing Xcode into the search box window.

1. Choose **File | Open** or *Command + O*.
2. Double-click into the **MapKitExample** folder, and select the **MapKitExample.xcodeproj** file.

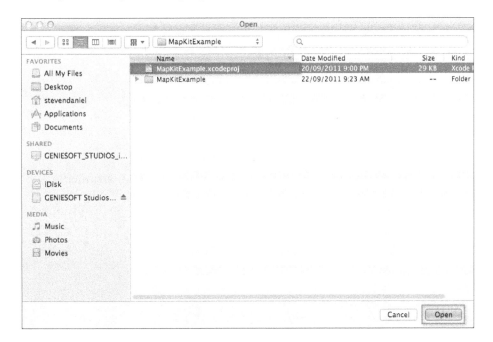

3. Click on the **Open** button to continue to load and open the file into the Xcode workspace environment.

We now need to start running and profiling our application, which will be used to perform a system trace on what threads and systems calls are being processed.

Running and profiling the project

To run the Instruments application from within the Xcode environment, select the **Build For Profiling** option under the **Build For** menu, or by using the keyboard shortcut *Shift + Command + I*, and then select the **Profile** option from the **Product** menu to launch the Instruments application. Similarly, you can use the keyboard shortcut *Command + I*.

Once this option has been selected, you will eventually see the Instruments application window display on your screen. This is shown in the following screenshot:

The following table gives an overview of each of the templates available, and required for iOS development:

Template	Description
Blank	Creates an empty trace document to which you can add your own combinations of instruments.
Time Profiler	Performs low-overhead and time-based sampling of one or all processes.
System Trace	Provides you with the ability to profile against different aspects of the operating system which could be affecting application performance.
Activity Monitor	This monitors overall CPU, memory, disk, and network activity.
Automation	Automates user interface tests within your application.

Template	Description
Energy Diagnostics	Displays diagnostics information regarding the amount of energy being used on the device for GPU activity, display brightness, sleep/wake, bluetooth, Wi-Fi, and GPS.
Network Connections	With this instrument, it's possible to see how much data is flowing over each connection, for each application, as well as interesting statistics, such as round trip times and retransmission requests. You can use this information to help reduce network traffic and energy consumption.
Allocations	Monitors memory and object-allocation patterns within your program.
Leaks	Detects memory leaks within your application.
Threads	Analyzes thread state transitions within a process, including running and terminated threads, thread state, and associated back traces.
File Activity	Monitors an application's interaction with the file system.

The type of instrument that we want to use for this example is the **System Trace Instrument**. Select the **System Trace** option and then click on the **Profile** button to proceed to load the **Instruments Trace Document** window, and start profiling our `MapKitExample` application.

Your application will then be analyzed, and each system call and thread that has been made to memory will be profiled. These also include **Virtual Memory (VM)** operations.

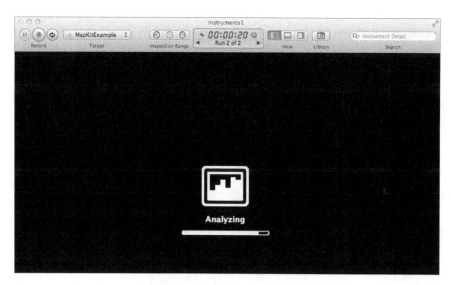

You will notice that after a number of seconds have passed, your trace information is displayed. This contains information relating to the thread and system calls, and their duration that your application is currently making. Other information, such as Virtual VM faults, is also recorded.

You can choose to stop the application from profiling by clicking on the red record button, since the Instruments application has already done its full analysis.

The following list items shows the comparison between the various different types of faults you will encounter while developing iOS applications, along with their explanations.

VM faults

Virtual memory (**VM**) is an auxiliary storage that is located on a computer's hard disk that the operating system uses when the **Random Access Memory** (**RAM**) is full. It used for all normal computer applications. Many computers do not have their virtual memory set properly, and as a result, are not getting maximum performance, resulting in a system fault.

Memory leaks

A **memory leak** occurs when memory is allocated by an application, but never released.

Let's take a closer look at the following example:

```
for (int i = 1; I <= 500; i++) {
  NSString *MemStatus = [[NSString alloc]
  initWithFomat:@"Memory allocating..."];
}
```

In this code snippet, we allocate 500 strings inside a loop to demonstrate ways in which memory leaks can happen. The code allocates memory for each new string MemStatus each time it goes through the loop, and lets the pointer to each string that gets allocated go out of scope. As you can see, the memory that gets allocated never gets released, causing your application to run slowly, and even potentially causing it to crash or simply hang.

Run-time errors

These types of errors cause your application to stop executing. It can be caused by an unhandled exception due to an *out of memory* issue, or *you are writing some data out to a database*, or *you may have exceeded the maximum allowable size that a field can handle*.

Compile-time errors

These types of errors are the most obvious, simply because your program will not compile (and therefore won't run) until all of them are fixed. Generally, these come from typographical errors.

The Objective-C compile in Xcode is case-sensitive, which means that `UIcolor` and `UIColor` are treated differently. For example, in Objective-C, the compiler can understand the following:

```
self.view.backgroundColor = [UIColor blueColor];
```

But if you type in:

```
self.view.backgroundColor = [UIColor bluecolor];
```

The compiler will call it a compile-time error, because you've specified a language-specific (syntax) that it can't recognize.

The **Trace Highlights** section of the Instruments window shows a set of useful graphs, based on the information that has been profiled. It contains graphs that show the overall usage used by the system, as well as the number of Threads and System calls, and VM calls.

Each of the colors within this view indicates information related to each of the different tracks, and to which library each method belongs. Single-clicking on any of the charts will take you into a summary view, showing an overall break-down into each section, including call stack views, duration, and so on.

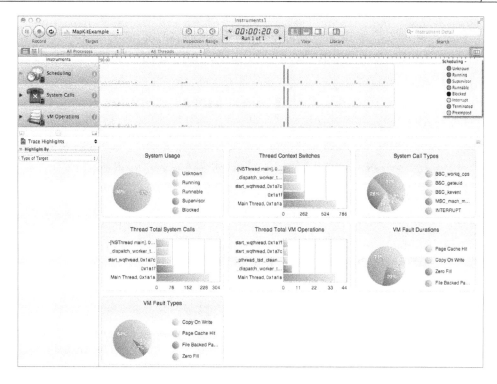

There is also the ability to change and have each of the chart colors displayed in a different color. This can be done by clicking on the **Scheduling** button icon, as shown in this screenshot.

To change any of the colors, click on each color from the pop-up list. This will display the color wheel to the left of the instruments window, where you can change the corresponding color value within the color wheel provided.

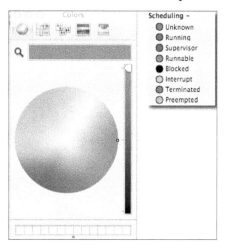

In this section, we looked at how to go about running and profiling an existing project using the Instruments application to help track-down issues with performance within our application, by using the System Trace for iOS instrument.

We looked at the different views available within the Instruments application, and how to represent the trace document results as a color-coded graph through the Trace Highlights view, to indicate which section each method belongs to.

Adding and configuring Instruments

The Instruments application comes with a wide-range of built-in instruments to make your job easier, by using them to gather data from one or more processes. Most of these instruments require little configuration to use, and are simply added to your trace document to start gathering trace data. We will look at how we add and configure instruments into an existing trace document.

Using the Instruments library

The Instruments library displays all the instruments that you can use and add to your trace document. The library contains all of the built-in instruments that come with the installation of Xcode 4, as well as any custom instruments that you have already created.

To open the **Instruments** window, click on the **Library** button from within your trace document window or choose **Window | Library** from the menu bar. Alternatively, you can use the *Command + L* keyboard shortcut.

As you can see from this screenshot, the Instruments **Library** list contains a massive number of instruments, which can grow over time especially when you start adding your own custom-built instruments.

The library list provides several options for organizing and finding the instrument that you are looking for, by using the different view modes. **View modes** help you to decide the amount of information that should be displayed at any one time, and the amount of space you want that instrument group to occupy.

In the following table, we describe the view modes supported by the Instruments **Library**.

View mode types	Description
View Icons	This setting displays only the icon representing each instrument
View Icons And Labels	This setting displays the icon with the name of the instrument
View Icons And Descriptions	This setting displays the icon, name, and full description of each of the instruments
View Small Icons And Labels	This setting displays the name of the instrument, with a small version of its icon

In addition to setting the view mode of the Instruments **Library**, instruments can be organized into groups, which makes it easier to identify which instrument relates to which group. This is shown in the previous screenshot.

Locating an Instrument within the Library

There are two ways to locate an instrument within the Instrument **Library**. One common way is to use the group selection criteria controls, which is located at the top of the **Library** window, and can be used to select one or more groups to limit the amount of instruments that are displayed within the **Library** window.

If you drag the split bar between the pop-up menu and the instrument pane downwards, you will notice that the pop-up menu changes from a single selection to an outline view, so that you can select multiple groups, by holding down the *Command* key combinations, and then selecting the desired groups to display with your mouse, as shown in the following screenshot:

Another way to filter the contents of the Instruments **Library** window is to use the **Search** field, which is located at the bottom of the **Library** window. By using this **Search** field, you can quickly narrow-down and display only those instruments that have the search keyword within their name, description, category, list, or keywords.

In the following screenshot, all instruments that contain the search string `file` are displayed.

Adding and removing instruments

There will be times when you want to trace your application against other instruments within the Instruments **library**. This could be because you want to check to see how your application is performing on the device, and how much battery is being consumed by your application.

You can add as many instruments to your trace document as you wish, but be aware that not all instruments included in the library are capable of tracking a wide-range of system processes; you will find that some can only track a single process. To get around this, you can add multiple instances of the instrument, and assign each one to a different process. By doing it this way, you gather similar information for multiple programs running simultaneously.

To add an instrument to the trace document, select the instrument from the Instrument **Library**, and then drag it either to the **Instruments** pane or directly onto the track pane of your trace document, as shown in the following screenshot:

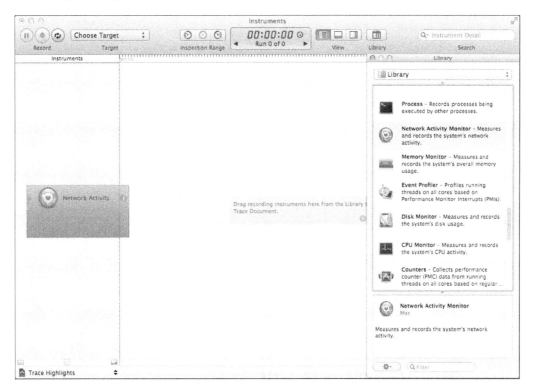

To remove an instrument from the trace document, select the instrument that you would like to remove from the **Instruments** pane, and then press the *Delete* key on your keyboard. You will then receive a confirmation message. Click on the **OK** button to proceed.

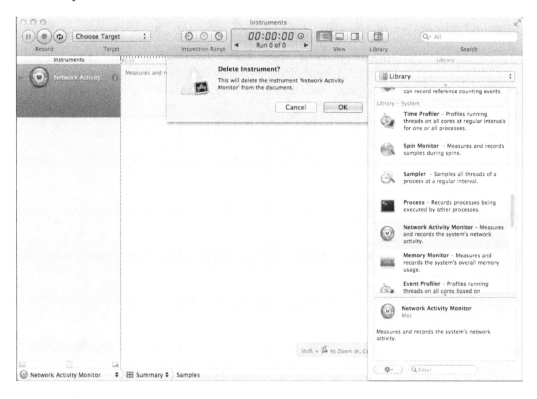

In the next section, we will look at how we go about configuring an instrument that you have added to your trace document.

Configuring an instrument

You will find that most of the instruments that you add to your trace document are ready-to-use, out of the box. However, some instruments can be configured using the **Instruments Inspector** and vary depending on the type of instrument being configured.

You will notice that most instruments contain options for configuring the contents of the track pane, while only a small handful contain additional functionality for determining what type of information is gathered by the instrument. To configure an instrument, select the instrument from the **Instruments** pane and then click on the **Instrument Inspector Icon**, which is located to the right of the instrument. This is shown in the following screenshot:

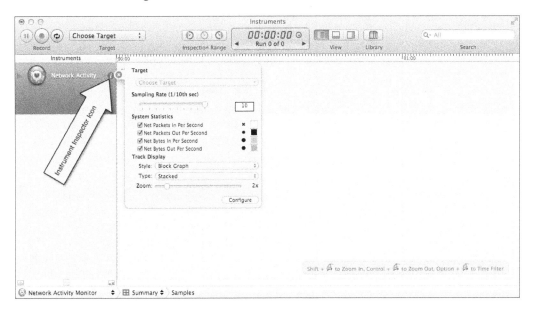

When the **Instrument Inspector Icon** is clicked, it displays the inspector configuration dialog box next to the instrument name. To dismiss the inspector, click on the close button highlighted by an **X**. You can similarly use the *Command + I* and **File | Get Info** commands to close this window also. Depending on the type of instrument that is being configured, they can either be configured before, during, or after the data within your trace document has been recorded.

The **Zoom** control can be found in most of the inspector controls for those instruments, which you configure. This feature controls the magnification of the trace data that is displayed within the track pane, and adjusts the height of the instrument within the track pane. Alternatively, you can use the **View | Decrease Deck Size** and **View | Increase Deck Size** menu options to do the same thing.

Other components of the Instruments family explained

There are other instruments, which come with the Instruments application, apart from tracking down memory leaks and allocation objects. Although not every instrument works with iOS applications, the list of instruments pertaining to which type is explained in the following table:

Instrument	Platform	Description
Activity Monitor	iOS /Simulator	Correlates the system workload with the virtual memory size.
Allocations	iOS / Simulator	This can be used to take snapshots of the heap, as applications perform their tasks. If taken at two different points in time, it can be used to identify situations where memory is being lost, not leaked.
		The test case would be to take a snapshot, do something in the application, and then undo that something, returning the state of the application to its prior point. If the memory allocated in the heap is the same, no worries. It's a simple and repeatable test scenario of performing a task, and returning the application to its state prior to performing the task.
Automation	iOS / Simulator	Used to automate user interface tests in your iOS application.
Core Animation	iOS	Measures the number of Core Animation frames-per-second in a process running on an iOS device, through visual hints that help you understand how content is rendered on the screen.
CPU Sampler	iOS / Simulator	Correlates the overall system workload with the work being done specifically by your application.
Energy Diagnostics	iOS	Displays diagnostics information regarding the amount of energy being used on the device for GPU activity, display brightness, sleep/wake, bluetooth, WiFi, and GPS.

Instrument	Platform	Description
File Activity	Simulator	Examines file usage patterns in the system, by monitoring when files open, close, read, and write operations to files. It also monitors changes in the file system itself, relating to permission and owner changes.
Leaks	iOS / Simulator	This instrument looks for situations where memory has been allocated, but is no longer able to be used. These memory leaks can lead to the application crashing or being shut-down.
OpenGL ES Driver	iOS	Determines how efficiently you are using OpenGL and the GPU on iOS devices.
System Usage	iOS	Records calls to functions that operate on files within a process on the iOS device.
Threads	Simulator	Analyzes state transitions within a process, including both running and terminating threads, thread state, and associated back traces.
Time Profiler	iOS / Simulator	Performs low-overhead and time-based sampling of one or all processes.
Zombies	Simulator	The Zombies instrument keeps an empty or 'dead' object alive (in a sense) in place of objects that have already been released. These 'dead' objects are later accessed by the faulty application logic and halt execution of the application without crashing. The 'zombie' objects receive the call, and point the instrument to the exact location where the application would normally crash.

What's new in Instruments

The Instruments application which comes with Xcode contains a wide range of built-in instruments to make your job easier, and to gather and display data for one or more processes. In Xcode 4.2, a collection of new instruments has been added and these are explained as follows.

Time Profiler with CPU strategy

The **Time profiler instrument** illustrates how much time is being spent in each code segment. This allows developers to prioritize which bit of logic needs to be re-factored prior to release. Although this can be run using the iOS simulator, it is recommended to run this on the iOS devices, as the performance will vary greatly between the two.

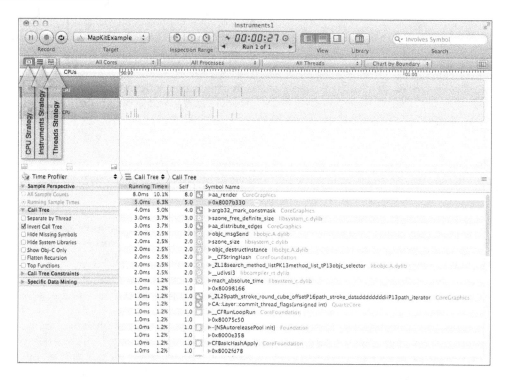

Within the Time Profiler instrument, you can use the buttons at the left end of this bar to display the track view pane, using one of three strategies shown in the following table:

View mode types	Description
CPU strategy	This setting displays CPU activity on each active core. This strategy can help you determine if your application has achieved concurrency.
Instruments strategy	This setting displays CPU activity in a single track. This is the default strategy.
Threads strategy	This setting displays the CPU activity per-individual-thread.

The Time Profiler instrument also provides developers with the ability to run the applications that they are developing on the iPad 2 and iPhone 4/4S. You can use the CPU strategy feature to measure activity on each CPU core.

This is highlighted by the red rectangle, show in the previous screenshot. If your application supports concurrency, this should show evidence of activity on both of the iPad 2 cores at the same time.

 The CPU strategy feature is currently only available in the Time Profiler instrument.

There is also the ability to configure the Time Profiler instrument to limit the number of active processor cores. This is to allow you to configure your application to see how it will perform on systems running with fewer cores. An example of this would be, for instance, if you had a MacBook Pro running with four active core processors, but you wanted to limit this to work with two active core processors, to see how this would profile on a MacBook Pro running two cores.

If your CPU supports multi-threading, this is also referred to as **hyper-threading**. This means that for each physical core, there is a second logical core. Take for example: if you have a system that has hyper-threading enabled, and running with four physical cores, this will result in the system running with a total of eight cores.

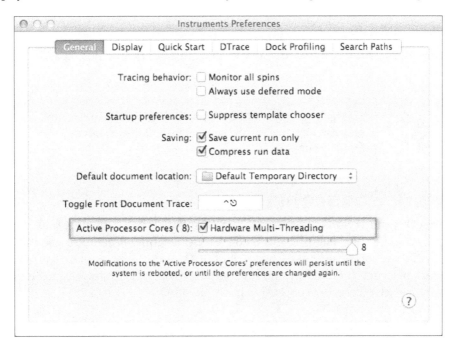

This screenshot shows you how to go about configuring the total number of active-processor cores. This screen can be accessed through the **Instruments | Preferences** menu option, or alternatively, you can use the *Command* + key combination.

From this screen, click on the **General** pane, and then select or deselect the **Hardware Multi-Threading** checkbox from the **Active Processor Cores**, provided that this feature is supported by your system. You can also use the slider to specify the number of active cores to use.

> Any changes made to the number of active cores doesn't turn off any of the processor cores-instead, the Instruments application tells the system not to schedule work on the cores that are made inactive.

System Trace for iOS

The **System Trace for iOS** instrument gives you the ability to profile against different aspects of the operating system which could be affecting application performance. This provides information on any system calls, thread scheduling, and **Virtual Memory (VM)** operations.

An example of where this instrument could be useful, would be when you want to find out why your code is not executing on the CPU in a timely fashion, or if you are a game developer, and you wanted to find out why your applications, frame-rate has dropped unexpectedly.

In Instruments 4.2, you can use the System Trace tool to profile both iOS and Mac OS X.

> For more information on how to use this type of instrument, refer to the section named *Tracing iOS applications*, located within this chapter.

Network Connections

The **Network Connections** instrument gives you the ability to inspect how your iOS application is using TCP/IP and UDP/IP connections. When you use this instrument, it automatically takes a snapshot of all open ports available, and reports their cumulative network activity within the detail view, to see how much data is flowing over each connection and for each application.

The following screenshot displays the **Connection Summary** section of the detail view, and shows the incoming and outgoing network connections, as well as all of the open connections for all processes.

You will also see that you are provided with the ability to view statistic, such as round trip times and re-transmission requests to help reduce network traffic and energy consumption.

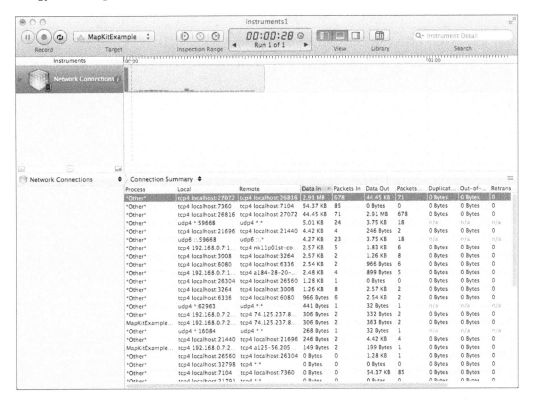

The detail view also allows you to choose from the following display views; these are explained in the following table:

View mode types	Description
Process summary	This setting aggregates the cumulative data for each process only.
Interface summary	This setting aggregates the data by network.

You can also choose to have the details view display a set of useful graphs, by selecting the **Trace Highlights** option, as shown in the following screenshot:

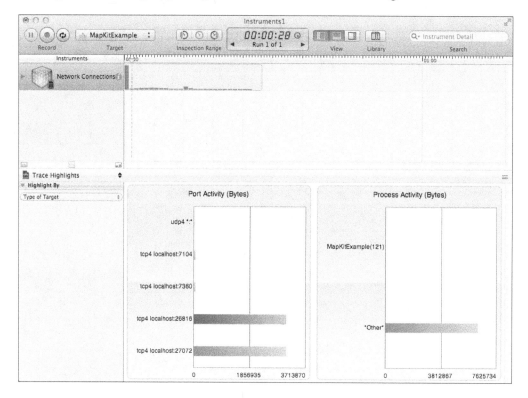

This screenshot shows the **Port Activity** and the **Process Activity** comparisons. The **Port Activity** feature measures the incoming and outgoing connections. The **Process Activity** feature measures the activity used by the application.

Network activity

The **Network Activity** instrument helps you bridge the gap between networking (cellular and Wi-Fi) and energy usage. You can use this instrument to track the device-wide volume of data flow through each network interface alongside an energy usage level taken directly from the battery, as well as correlate network activity with energy usage in iOS devices, and is also included as part of the Energy Diagnostics template for iOS.

The following screenshot displays the **Energy Diagnostics** trace document, with the run results that show the different **Energy Usage** levels:

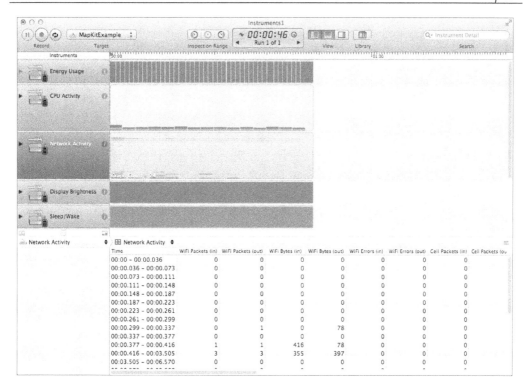

When you run this for the first time, you will notice that the network activity is frequent enough to keep the process active, which will result in much greater energy consumption. If you were to run this again, you will notice that the same data is transmitted in larger, but less frequent bursts, allowing the application to sleep between transmissions.

The **Energy Diagnostics** instrument is the most exciting tool that Apple gave to developers. This instrument will help you identify optimum use of the iOS device resources, by enabling you to test your application as close to real-world scenarios as possible.

The data collected can later be analyzed to see how much of the device's battery life each function consumes, and it will tell the developer how long each of the device's various components are used. If you need to know the user's location, it will tell you which devices were turned on and for how long. **GPS** is a particular resource that consumes much of the device's battery life. Turning off **location services** once a location has been obtained is ideal.

If you are interested in reading more about Instruments, you can refer to the *Instruments User Guide Documentation*, at the following link provided: `http://developer.apple.com/library/ios/#documentation/DeveloperTools/Conceptual/InstrumentsUserGuide/Introduction/Introduction.html`.

Summary

In this chapter, we focused on the new additions to the Xcode Instruments application, and how we can use this brilliant tool to ensure that our application runs smoothly, free from bottlenecks that could potentially affect the performance of an application.

We took a look into each of the different types of built-in instruments that become part of the Instruments application, in particular the Systems Trace for iOS instrument. This helps track-down system calls, memory, and threads that may be affecting application performance on your iOS applications.

We ended the chapter looking at how we can configure instruments to represent data differently within the trace document.

I hope you have enjoyed reading it as much as I did writing it. This is certainly not the end of the road for you. There is a lot of stuff to explore in the world of Xcode and iPhone. Don't worry! You won't be on your own. There are many developers out there who are more than willing to help you in case you get stuck at any point in time: `http://developer.apple.com/devforums/`.

Good luck with your Xcode journey. I hope to see your application on the Apple App Store soon!

Index

H

Hardware Multi-Threading checkbox **218**
HideWireframe option **73**
Home screen **35**
Hybrid view **172**
hyper-threading **217**

I

IBAction event **105**
IBAction method **98**
iCloud
  backup **47-50**
  documents, storing **39, 40**
  documents, using **39, 40**
  documents, working with **61**
  file-version conflicts, cause of action **62**
  file-version conflicts, handling **62**
  Google Docs, comparing **39**
  key-valued data, storing **41, 42**
iCloud backup
  iCloudExample application, creating **51-57**
iCloudExample application
  creating **50-57**
iCloud storage
  APIs **58-61**
  document, moving **57**
  entitlements, requesting **42-47**
  using **63**
image filter effects, applying to CIImage
    class
  about **146**
  color effects **148-155**
  transitions **156-158**
imageWithCGImage method **155**
iMessage
  about **30, 31**
  advantages **31**
iMessage application **10**
inputAmount property **150**
inputAngle property **153**
Inspection Range control **198**
installing
  iOS 5 SDK **11-14**
instantiateViewControllerWithIdentifier
    method **113**
instrument

adding **210, 211**
components **214, 215**
configuring **212, 213**
features **215-220**
locating, within library **208-210**
removing **210, 212**
instrument configuration
  Instruments library, using **206-208**
Instrument Inspector Icon **213**
Instruments
  about **195, 196**
  adding **206**
  compile-time errors **204, 205**
  configuring **206**
  Instruments pane **197**
  MapKitExample project, loading **199, 200**
  memory leaks **203**
  Navigation bar **197**
  Run-time errors **204**
  trace document toolbar **197**
  VM faults **203**
Instruments Inspector **212**
instruments trace document toolbar
  Loop button **198**
  Pause/Resume button **198**
IntegratedDevelopmentEnvironment (IDE)
  14
interface builder
  about **168**
  storyboard files, creating **169**
Interface summary **219**
iOS 5
  about **7**
  ARC **8**
  features **8**
  iMessage **7**
  Notification Center **7**
  SDK, installing **11-14**
iOS 5 SDK
  components, Instruments **14**
  components, iOSSimulator **14**
  components, Xcode **14**
  installing **14**
  SDK, installing **11-14**
iOSApplicationProgrammingGuide **50**
iOS applications
  tracing **199**

Thank you for buying
iOS 5 Essentials

About Packt Publishing

Packt, pronounced 'packed', published its first book "*Mastering phpMyAdmin for Effective MySQL Management*" in April 2004 and subsequently continued to specialize in publishing highly focused books on specific technologies and solutions.

Our books and publications share the experiences of your fellow IT professionals in adapting and customizing today's systems, applications, and frameworks. Our solution based books give you the knowledge and power to customize the software and technologies you're using to get the job done. Packt books are more specific and less general than the IT books you have seen in the past. Our unique business model allows us to bring you more focused information, giving you more of what you need to know, and less of what you don't.

Packt is a modern, yet unique publishing company, which focuses on producing quality, cutting-edge books for communities of developers, administrators, and newbies alike. For more information, please visit our website: www.packtpub.com.

Writing for Packt

We welcome all inquiries from people who are interested in authoring. Book proposals should be sent to author@packtpub.com. If your book idea is still at an early stage and you would like to discuss it first before writing a formal book proposal, contact us; one of our commissioning editors will get in touch with you.

We're not just looking for published authors; if you have strong technical skills but no writing experience, our experienced editors can help you develop a writing career, or simply get some additional reward for your expertise.

iOS Development using MonoTouch Cookbook

ISBN: 978-1-84969-146-8   Paperback: 384 pages

109 simple but incredibly effective recipes for developing and deploying applications for iOS using C# and .NET

1. Detailed examples covering every aspect of iOS development using MonoTouch and C#/.NET

2. Create fully working MonoTouch projects using step-by-step instructions

3. Recipes for creating iOS applications meeting Apple's guidelines

Cocos2d for iPhone 0.99 Beginner's Guide

ISBN: 978-1-84951-316-6   Paperback: 368 pages

Make mind-blowing 2D games for iPhone with this fast, flexible, and easy-to-use framework!

1. A cool guide to learning cocos2d with iPhone to get you into the iPhone game industry quickly

2. Learn all the aspects of cocos2d while building three different games

3. Add a lot of trendy features such as particles and tilemaps to your games to captivate your players

4. Full of illustrations, diagrams, and tips for building iPhone games, with clear step-by-step instructions and practical examples

Please check **www.PacktPub.com** for information on our titles

www.ingramcontent.com/pod-product-compliance
Lightning Source LLC
La Vergne TN
LVHW062312060326
832902LV00013B/2175